THE CARNEGIE NOBODY KNOWS

By George Swetnam*

E VERYBODY KNOWS about Andrew Carnegie: He was the man who gave away libraries.[1] Someone a little more knowledgeable might say that Carnegie was a Scottish immigrant who started his career as a bobbin boy, then made millions in steel in some mysterious way while others were going broke in the same field, and gave much of it away.

Most historians who have paid him any attention know that Carnegie made his first important money in oil, not iron. During the oil excitement late in 1861, Carnegie invested about $11,000 in the Storey Farm in the Oil Creek valley. Costing $40,000, it repaid his share more than $17,000 the first year and eventually returned a total of more than $5 million.[2] One biographer asserts with no basis of fact that the investment was on credit and was paid for from the dividends.[3] Another, who had access to Carnegie's papers and was a careful researcher, states that the shares were paid for with profits from the Woodruff sleeping cars.[4] Winkler also states, quite without proof, that some of the $30 million of bonds Carnegie sold overseas "turned out to be worthless as October leaves."[5] Quite the contrary, much of Carnegie's success and the profit he turned in selling securities came from his reputation for handling only good ones.

But every biographer, including his latest who has written the only good one on him, has proved virtually oblivious to one important side of the industrialist: his literary ability. Burton K. Hendrick mentions most of Carnegie's books and includes a partial and inaccurate list

* The author, a retired journalist and historian, lives in Glenshaw, Pennsylvania. This paper was presented at the annual meeting of the Pennsylvania Historical Association at Westminster College in 1975.

1. Even official Carnegie corporation estimates differ as to how many, but the most commonly accepted number is 2,811.

2. Joseph F. Wall, *Andrew Carnegie* (New York, 1970), p. 176.

3. John K. Winkler, *Incredible Carnegie* (New York, 1931), p. 85.

4. Burton K. Hendrick, *The Life of Andrew Carnegie* (New York, 1932), 1:123.

5. Winkler, *Incredible Carnegie*, p. 105.

of his magazine articles and published speeches in his appendix. But he never seems to realize either Carnegie's importance as a writer or his literary impact on the world in which he lived.[6] Except for a few instances, he seems to look upon Carnegie's writing as an innocent and sometimes profitable hobby.

Joseph Wall mentions only a few of Carnegie's literary works and is almost oblivious to this important side of his subject. During an interview shortly after the appearance of his splendid biography, I happened to mention that Twayne Press had commissioned me to write a book on Carnegie for its United States Authors Series[7]. He seemed surprised, saying, "I remember he wrote a little, but never realized it was of much importance."

"Before his stature as a steelman had made him widely known outside the Pittsburgh area and the industry," I replied, "he was one of the most sought-after writers for the top British and American reviews, such as *Forum, Contemporary Review, North American Review, Nineteenth Century* and the like. He wrote eight books,[8] all successfully published, and they were translated into French, German, Swedish, Hungarian, Spanish, Italian, and other languages."[9]

Wall's jaw dropped, and he said, "I didn't know that." But far from being irritated, this splendid scholar provided me with useful help, including typescripts of Carnegie material in United States Steel Corporation files, which were opened briefly for him and are now indefinitely closed to scholars.

Worse still, in a review of R. G. McCloskey's excellent *American Conservatism in the Age of Enterprise*,[10] Fritz Redlich criticized the author

6. Hendrick, *Carnegie*, 2:389–392. He lists with some errors the eight books published under Carnegie's name, but only about one-half the articles and printed speeches I have been able to locate for my forthcoming book. Indeed, I doubt if even my list includes them all.

7. Hopefully it will be published in the near future. It is waiting its turn in this busy series.

8. *Round the World* (n.p. [New York], 1879), revised and published by Scribner's (New York, 1884); *Our Coaching Trip*, (n.p. [New York], 1882), revised and published by Scribner's, (New York, 1883) as *An American Four-in-Hand in Britain; Triumphant Democracy*, (New York and London, 1886), revised and reissued, (New York and London, 1893); *The Gospel of Wealth*, (New York, 1900); *The Empire of Business*, (New York, 1902); *James Watt*, (Edinburgh, London and New York, 1905; *Problems of Today* (New York, 1908); *Autobiography of Andrew Carnegie* edited by John C. Van Dyke (Boston, 1920).

9. *National Union Catalog of Pre-1956 Imprints* (Chicago and London, 1968) German, 96; French, 25 et passim; Spanish, Dano-Norwegian, 27 et passim; Polish, 28; Greek, Swedish, Hungarian, 29; Esperanto, 30; Italian, Dutch, 31.

10. (Cambridge, Mass., 1951).

magazine - 24 intro
Triumphant Democracy
1889 Gospel of Wealth   exp.
a true liberal
greatest writer

THE CARNEGIE NOBODY KNOWS

p 34 not plutocracy - but culture
44 tho never religion - less so after
would tour '75 - all religions have truth
49 - time spent writing - travels -
38 rainy days

By GEORGE SWETNAM

and

HELENE SMITH

p 53 Gladstone in his Politics led him 1881-85 set up a
syndicate of radical newspapers to support
Gladstone + eliminate monarchy + House of Lords
- but little writing at this time

p 54 most fruitful part field of literature -
contributing to the magazines

Gospel of Wealth p 58 - worldwide prominence

I DO NOT WISH TO BE REMEMBERED BY
WHAT I GAVE BUT WHAT I HAVE PERSUADED
OTHERS TO GIVE - p 150
- ROCKEFELLERS SPECIALTY
- PURCHASING PEACE - SIMPLIFIED SPELLING
BOARD
1903 - 1915

152 →

ANDROO CARNAGIE
25,000 + YEAR - GAVE UP

Carnegie Inst. p 150
library, concert hall,
museum, art gallery

+ a craft school for
workmen which in
1912 became a
college + now is
Carnegie-Mellon U.

HERO FUND - 152
- "peace as well as
war had heroes"

1910 - established
the Carnegie
A foundation
give away
rest $125,000
154

McDONALD/SWARD
PUBLISHING
COMPANY

had given
away 180,000
but still
had as
much left

Revised Edition
Copyright © 1989 George Swetnam and Helene Smith
All Rights Reserved
Library of Congress Catalog Card Number: 89-60700

Printed in the United States of America
McDonald/Swärd Publishing Company
ISBN 0-945437-07-2

Copyright ©1980 by G. K. Hall & Co.
ANDREW CARNEGIE
Published in 1980 by Twayne Publishers,
A Division of G. K. Hall & Co.
All Rights Reserved

Library of Congress Cataloging in Publication Data

Swetnam, George.
Andrew Carnegie.

(Twayne's United States authors series; TUSAS 355)
Bibliography: pp. 173–78
Includes index.
1. Carnegie, Andrew, 1835-1919.
2. Steel industry and trade—United States—Biography.
3. Authors, American—19th century—Biography.
HD9515.5.C37S83   338.7′67′20924 [B]   79-17472
ISBN 0-8057-7239-1

for saying or implying that the ideas expressed by Carnegie in his *Triumphant Democracy* were his own.

> When a wealthy and powerful American business leader "writes" a book or pamphlet, the assumption is that he hired a ghost writer.
>
> In the case of Carnegie we know (at least for the period in which *Triumphant Democracy* was written) who the ghost writer was: James Howard Bridge . . . had been Herbert Spencer's secretary from 1879 to 1884. In the latter year he became Carnegie's "literary assistant,"[11] resigning from that post in 1889. How much he contributed to the *Forum* essays in 1886 and to *Triumphant Democrary*, and in turn how great was Carnegie's share therein is not known to the reviewer, nor does he know who Carnegie's later "literary assistants" were. . . . In this case the line runs from Spencer to Bridge, then to Bridge plus Carnegie. . . .
>
> Bridge . . . may have had a more than fifty per cent share in the book, and a considerable influence on Carnegie's thinking, the latter thereby absorbing Spencerism.[12]

This criticism shows a staggering ignorance of or disregard for the period in which the writing in question occurred. There were as yet no ghost writers, and Carnegie was the first modern American businessman who could properly be called a writer. Furthermore, Carnegie was an announced Spencerian by 1870 (when Bridge was only fourteen years of age) and in 1882 he and Spencer were close friends.[13]

Oddly enough, while Wall,[14] Edward Kirkland,[15] and others have questioned and rejected such suggestions of ghost writing and strongly asserted that both internal and external evidence support Carnegie's authorship, I have found no one who pointed out how utterly impossible and ridiculous Redlich's arguments really are.

For a man so busy at making money as he was, Carnegie did an amazing amount of writing, including two books of travel,[16] both of

11. I have been unable to find any evidence that Bridge or anyone else ever held such a title or post. Bridge made no such claim. Carnegie always refers to him as his "secretary."

12. *American Historical Review*, 57 (April 1952):707–708.

13. Wall, *Carnegie*, pp. 381–383.

14. Interview referred to above.

15. *The Gospel of Wealth etc.*, edited by Edward C. Kirkland (Cambridge Mass., 1962), introduction, xix.

16. *Round the World* and *Our Coaching Trip*.

which he completely revised; a biography and an autobiography;[17] four on economics and politics;[18] and probably one on railroad telegraphy.[19] Also he penned almost seventy important magazine articles, more than seventy-five speeches which were published in pamphlet form, and hundreds of highly important letters, most of them—unfortunately—still unpublished, and some unavailable for study.[20]

Carnegie corresponded with six presidents,[21] who often appear to have taken his advice, and with British and American statesmen on internal and foreign policy. During the Spanish-American War (one of only three of which he ever approved) he cabled General Nelson Miles in Cuba, "Withdraw Santiago. Proceed full force to Porto Rico." Miles laid the advice before McKinley, got his approval, and did as Carnegie advised.[22] Carnegie also corresponded with other world leaders including King Edward VII, Kaiser Wilhelm II, and William E. Gladstone.[23]

We even know how Carnegie wrote—usually on a pad on his knee, using a stub pencil. His style was crisp and interesting, often sententious and argumentative, and his ideas were mostly liberal for his day.

From mid-teens, in correspondence with an uncle and cousin in Scotland, Carnegie wrote not only to express his ideas, but to convince others that they were right. This habit of correspondence he kept up almost until his death. In early youth he turned his pen (or pencil) to securing private actions he desired and influencing the public[24] through published speeches and writing letters to newspapers, another practice he kept up all his life.

But in the wider field of authorship he began with travel writing,

17. *James Watt* and *The Autobiography of Andrew Carnegie*, which was very badly edited by John C. Van Dyke.

18. *Triumphant Democracy, The Gospel of Wealth, The Empire of Business,* and *Problems of Today.*

19. *Rules for the Government of the Pennsylvania Railroad Company's Telegraph.* Earliest known edition, perhaps first, (Harrisburg, Pa., 1863).

20. In the limestone cavern archives of United States Steel Corporation, referred to above.

21. They were Benjamin Harrison, Grover Cleveland, William McKinley, Theodore Roosevelt, William Howard Taft, and Woodrow Wilson. Hendrick, *Carnegie,* 1:407, 428; 2:274–276, 303–339, 379–380.

22. Nelson A. Miles, *Serving the Republic,* (New York, 1911), p. 274.

23. Hendrick, *Carnegie,* 1:271–273, 280, 344–345, 355; 2:172, 298–316, et passim.

24. Carnegie, *Autobiography,* pp. 30–62 et passim.

apparently inspired by his admiration for Bayard Taylor's *Views A-Foot.*[25] Taylor had financed his first journeys by writing for newspapers. When Carnegie planned a walking tour of Europe with two companions, he arranged to write travel letters to a journal in Pittsburgh.

So far as his correspondence and existing newspaper files (and these are pretty complete) indicate, Carnegie wrote only three such letters, all to the *Commercial*, of which two were published. The first, dated at Inverness, Scotland, 21 August 1865, deals with fish breeding. He was far ahead of his time in suggesting it would be a useful practice in Western Pennsylvania. But before launching into the subject, he devoted a paragraph to his philosophy of travel writing:

> Descriptive letters from abroad are now-a-days so readily prepared from the omnipresent guide books, which give not only dates and particulars, but pages, written in excellent style, upon the memories and associations which a visit calls forth, that one feels a laudable disinclination to seek such publicity as your columns would afford, for what the guide would mostly be entitled to the credit of. But what we saw yesterday is so utterly foreign to the domain of the professional *litterateur* that we are prompted to write you in regard to it, in the hope that the subject may receive some attention at home.

The letter is a careful and accurate report of a salmon hatchery near Perth, including the investment and profits. As a youth he had dreamed of becoming a newspaper reporter, and he proved that he would have been a good one, by featuring the local angles that would interest a regional paper. It ran to something like 1200 words and was published 11 September over his initials.

Eighteen days later Carnegie wrote to W. S. Haven, a printer, stationer, and news dealer, thanking him for sending the paper, and telling of another letter "giving you my views on Protection, a subject Mr. Brigham[26] is stirring up thoroughly and well. . . . Mr. Brigham, I suppose, will give my protection letter his care. It isn't the Pittsburgh doctrine, I know. . . ."[27] Apparently Brigham disapproved of the variation from the "Pittsburgh doctrine," for it never appeared.

25. Hendrick, *Carnegie*, 1:137.

26. C. D. Brigham, editor of the *Commercial*.

27. Travel letters in the collection of Margaret Carnegie Miller, typescript lent by J. F. Wall.

Carnegie's third and final letter to the *Commercial* is dated from Amsterdam, 15 November (although he was in Berlin by that time). Printed 13 December it was almost wholly devoted to the dikes and reclamation of land from the sea.

It was almost fifteen years later that Carnegie fell into commercial writing, almost by accident, with his first book. In 1878 he had taken an eight-month trip around the world, writing an account of his travels—first person and dated day by day in the manner of Taylor. But if he borrowed the format, that was the only thing. The writing and content are pure Carnegie. Reaching New York 24 June 1879, he wrote the two final paragraphs at Cresson (his summer home) the following day. He almost immediately had it printed (and there were numerous subsequent printings) by Charles Scribner's Sons, as a sort of thank-you gift to "my brother, and trusty associates, who toiled at home that I might spend abroad."

Three years later Carnegie took another trip (aside from his annual voyages to and from Europe) entertaining his mother and a group of friends on a coaching trip from Brighton to Inverness—almost the entire length of the island kingdom. He took only brief notes, but at twenty sittings on snowy days that winter turned out *Our Coaching Trip*, for private distribution.[28] It was also published by Scribner's, whose J. D. Champlin became interested, and suggested it might be revised for commercial distribution.

Carnegie took the revision seriously, making sixty-seven principal changes, including fifty-eight additions (mostly of guidebook-type material), three corrections, and six omissions—one of them a 53-page newspaper account of their stop at Dunfermline. In all, the length was increased by about one-third. The title became *An American Four-in-Hand in Britain*, and it was published in 1883. It was reprinted eighteen times and was still paying royalties in 1912.

The book's success suggested a revision of *Round the World*, which proved more extensive than that of its mate. Disregarding minor variations, it included 123 changes, of which eighty-eight were additions, twenty-six adaptations, and nine omissions. Only thirty-one of the additions were to insert guidebook-type material. The others were to advance his ideas, including twenty-two on economics and fifteen on religion. Even the guidebook material is significant, most of it being chosen to illustrate or prepare for his ideas. Although not so

28. Carnegie, *Autobiography*, p. 203.

successful as the former work, *Round the World* was reprinted at least eight times, through 1902.[29]

Carnegie's career as a magazine writer—which led to his highest glory in the writing field—came almost by accident. During his years as a lion in London he had formed a friendship with John Morley, editor of *Fortnightly Review*. While the coaching trip was creating much attention, a "noted politician" (never named) suggested, "Why don't you give us, in one of our reviews, some account of your coaching trip . . . and tell us what your dozen of American guests thought of us?" Carnegie passed the suggestion along to Morley, who approved it. But to everyone's surprise, instead of its being a sweet tribute to scenery, hospitality and other delights of the trip, Carnegie—who was beginning his drive to reform Britain and overthrow the monarchy—made it a bitter criticism of the political and social situation in the country. The solution, of course, was to change Britain into a republic.

Titled *As Others See Us*, the article appeared in *Fortnightly* in February 1882. Carnegie quickly prepared another for the same review, but in the meantime, Morley had gone into politics, being succeeded as editor by T. H. S. Escott. Apparently he rejected the article, and Carnegie never wrote for that review again.

In fact, he did not write for any magazine for nearly three years. A statistical compendium[30] and a conversation with Gladstone[31] launched him on *Triumphant Democracy*, a book designed to show that Britain's monarchical system, and those of other nations were holding them back, while democratic America was overtaking them and forging ahead on the economic front. He put his "clever secretary" to work gathering applicable facts and information, and within about three years completed the entire book of nearly 150,000 words—all his own writing except part of one chapter which he credited to Bridge, explaining why it was so used.

Perhaps from long association with newspapermen he had started each of his travel books with a "slam bang" opening like the "lead" of a spot news story. He followed the same custom with his third book:

> The old nations of the earth creep on at a snail's pace; the Republic thunders past with the rush of an express. The United States, the growth of a single century, has already reached the

29. Hendrick, *Carnegie*, 1:237.
30. M. G. Mulhall, *Balance Sheet of the World for Ten Years, 1870–1880*, (London, 1881).

foremost rank among nations, and is destined to outdistance all others in the race. In population, in wealth, in annual savings and in public credit; in freedom from debt, in agriculture, and in manufactures, America already leads the civilized world.

His first chapter was titled "The Republic," and he lost no time in presenting the argument that America's political system was at least the third most important factor in this achievement, and had benignly affected the other two—ethnic character and environment. The next eighteen compared the American people, cities and towns, conditions of life, occupations, education, religion, pauperism and crime rates, agriculture, manufactures, mining, trade and commerce, transportation, cultural advance, unity, foreign affairs, government, and finances with those of the older nations, in almost everything creditably to his adopted land. The final chapter reinforced his conclusions as stated in the opening one. The book is pure Carnegie. Much of its thesis and argument may be found in his boyhood letters to a cousin in Scotland thirty years previously.

Triumphant Democracy was a highly successful book. In the United States it went through four printings and sold more than 30,000 copies—a large sale in that day. In Britain it did almost as well in boards, besides a paperback edition whose sales passed 40,000 copies. It was translated into several languages, and sold all over Europe.[32]

Encouraged by this success, Carnegie completely revised the book following the 1890 census, with the subtitle changed from "Fifty" to "Sixty Years' March of the Republic." There was some moderation in his attacks on the British monarchy, but no significant change in the author's thinking. The second *Triumphant Democracy* is a better work than its predecessor, but somewhat heavier reading, and its sale never approached that of the first.

Even before the completion of work on *Triumphant Democracy*, Carnegie had returned to the magazine field with an article on the oil and gas wells of Pennsylvania, printed in *Macmillan's Magazine* early in 1885, and articles the following year in *North American Review* and the newly founded *Forum*, and *The Scottish Leader*.

Then came a hiatus of more than two years because of his bout with typhoid fever and the death of his mother and brother, all in the autumn of 1886, and his marriage the following April. But in 1889 Carnegie was back with five articles, and from then until stricken with

31. Carnegie, *Autobiography*, pp. 318–320.
32. Wall, *Carnegie*, pp. 442–444.

age twenty-five years later he averaged about three published articles a year.

The year 1889, however, marked his peak literary success: articles (or a two-part article) in the June and December *North American Review*, titled "Wealth" and "The Best Fields for Philanthropy." In them, Carnegie poured out his philosophy that the wealthy should give away their fortunes while still alive, and that to die rich is to die disgraced. Reprinted in England, it was titled *The Gospel of Wealth*,[33] and under this title it spread like wildfire over Europe, translated into many languages. In 1900 it was printed in book form along with other articles and an address, again under the British title, and became Carnegie's best known and most successful work. Many charged Carnegie with being insincere, but he lived up to his creed. By the time of his death in 1919 he had given away $311 million.[34]

Other groups of his articles and speeches appeared in book form in *The Empire of Business* (1902) and—with much new material, as *Problems of Today* (1908). Both were reasonably successful, despite the fact that much of their material had previously appeared in periodicals or in published addresses.

Two other works deserve notice: Soon after the turn of the century the Edinburgh firm of Oliphant, Anderson and Ferrier invited Carnegie to write a biography of James Watt for its Famous Scots series. He declined, saying that his thoughts were on other matters. But reflecting that Watt's inventions had paved the way to his own fortune, and that writing a book was the surest way to amend his lack of knowledge of his subject, Carnegie wrote the publishers again, offering to do the work. His *James Watt*, published in 1905, is interesting, though not a good biography. Reading between the lines, the public may learn more about Carnegie than Watt. It was a successful publication, however.

Carnegie employed much of his time in old age in writing notes for the *Autobiography*, already referred to. Unfortunately his failing memory and tendency to recall things as he wished they had been, together with Van Dyke's poor editing when it was brought out following the death of the industrialist, greatly detract from its value as a historical source. But it is charmingly written, and has been printed over and over again.

Carnegie was a man of his own day, with many of the faults

---

33. Kirkland, ed., *Gospel of Wealth*, 14n.

34. Ibid., introduction, xix. This was about 95% of his entire fortune.

and foibles of his fellows. Yet, despite the ill taste left by Homestead and the work of many detractors, he was a true liberal.

Much of what Carnegie wrote still has meaning for today and every day. And he not only had wide influence in setting the pattern of America's best period of journalism, but he initiated the development of one of the most important innovations in American letters—the vocal and literary industrialist and businessman. He was the first great American industrialist to be a writer, and the greatest writer of all principal industrialists.

Even on its merits alone, Carnegie's writing is worthy of a wider attention and acceptance than is accorded today. His style is crisp and attractive, and despite a tendency to moralize, was far better than the average American writing of its period. He avoided the artificiality and flights of fancy so common in that day, substituting plain fact and clear reasoning. Perhaps most important of all, he helped to frame and promote the American dream. He also, regrettably, forced businessmen who lacked his facility at expression to invent and foist on the public a new mouthpiece—the ghost writer.

The title, "The Carnegie Nobody Knows," first appeared on this article by George Swetnam for *Pennsylvania History*, Quarterly Journal of the Pennsylvania Historical Association, Vol. XLIV, No. 2—April, 1977.

Contents

Twayne's United States Authors Series

EDITOR OF THIS VOLUME

David J. Nordloh
Indiana University

Andrew Carnegie

Revised Edition
McDonald/Swärd Publishing Company
"Preservation Hill"
Box 104 A, RD 3
Greensburg, PA 15601

About the Authors

Recently retired after a distinguished career in journalism, George Swetnam has led an interesting life as a clergyman, commercial photographer, college teacher, hobo, newspaperman, historian, dramatist, and folklorist.

Born in Ohio of Kentucky mountaineer parents, he grew up in the deep South. He began his writing career early, and was listed in *Reader's Guide to Periodical Literature* while still in high school. After attending the University of South Carolina and University of Alabama, he graduated at the University of Mississippi, majoring in English. Entering Columbia Theological Seminary, Swetnam won the degree of Bachelor of Divinity with the highest grades in Hebrew in the school's 100-year history and was ordained a minister in the Presbyterian Church.

After holding pastorates in Alabama and Mississippi, he received a graduate fellowship from Auburn Theological Seminary (now merged with Union), where he received the degree of Master of Theology, majoring in Semitic Languages. He then attended Hartford Seminary Foundation, where he won his Ph.D. degree in Assyriology, his dissertation being a translation of 100 previously undeciphered Sumerian tablets from the Third Dynasty of Ur (about 2000 B.C.).

Following a second period in the pastorate, he taught English at the University of Alabama while taking two years of postdoctoral work in English and modern languages, founded a photographic firm, gave it away, and was a hobo for two years. Returning to respectable life, he edited a weekly newspaper in Tennessee, was managing editor of a daily in Pennsylvania, and became a columnist and feature writer for the *Pittsburgh Press*.

He is the author of a dozen books—including a three-volume history of Pittsburgh and the only history of transportation in Pennsylvania—and coauthor of a half a dozen more, as well as three produced historical dramas. He edited the *Keystone Folk-*

lore Quarterly for six years, founded the Institute of Pennsylvania Rural Life and Culture (now in its twenty-third year), and is a former member of the Council of the Pennsylvania Historical Association. Currently he is directing a comprehensive historical preservation survey under the auspices of the Pennsylvania Historical and Museum Commission. Outside the newspaper field his work has been widely published, principally in historical and literary journals.

Helene Snyder Smith is a native of western Pennsylvania. A graduate of Westminster College (PA), she began writing after her five children were in school and while engaged in historical archeology.

She is the author of *Getting Down to Earth*, a first-hand experience of an amateur archeologist; *Export, A Patch of Tapestry out of Coal Country America*, the history of a typical coal mining town; *Tavern Signs of America* (catalog and history); and (in collaboration with Swetnam) of *Hannah's Town, A Guidebook to Historic Western Pennsylvania*, and a number of successfully produced plays.

Smith is the principal author of three chapters (1, 3, 10) of this book (although it was originally, for contract purposes, published without her name) and contributed largely to most of the others.

Preface

Andrew Carnegie presents today's scholar with the paradox of an internationally known author whose writings have been almost totally eclipsed by his deeds. Ninety years ago, when he was just one among many American millionaire industrialists, his articles were welcomed by the best literary magazines on both sides of the Atlantic, his books were best sellers, and his writings were translated into many languages. His ideas influenced statesmen and scholars all over America and Europe. Today every school child recognizes his name as a steel-maker and philanthropist, but knows nothing he wrote except the *Autobiography*.

This situation has resulted in part from controversy over his character, controversy which has raged since the peak of his career. He has been held up as an angel or a devil, but seldom as the brilliant, ambitious, tender-hearted, puckish, and somewhat vain human being he was, with much the same virtues and vices as many of his contemporaries. And it has resulted from the rise of ghost writing, a development which has caused some historians to assume that his works were produced in that fashion.

The purpose of this study is to bring to American attention an outstanding author whose works have been neglected and even forgotten; to demonstrate that these are actually his own, the ideas and style following a consistent pattern from early youth to old age; and to point out the relation of his background and experiences to the ideas and attitudes evidenced in his writings.

To accomplish these purposes, the study will include only enough biographical material to throw a clear light on Carnegie's reasons and purposes in writing, and to demonstrate the more significant influences on his life, and how they affected his works. It will present a broad spectrum of his production in this respect, including a discussion of all his books, a wide selection of his articles and published speeches, and a few of his letters, against the background of their origin.

No attempt will be made to offer moral judgments on Carnegie's character or actions, or to excuse or explain away his ambivalence as a greedy businessman and an open-handed philanthropist and social reformer. Neither will the study enter into details regarding his economic and political beliefs. These are the concern of biography and technical treatises, not literary study.

Because of the diverse nature of Carnegie's writings, they will be taken up here in categorical and topical, rather than strictly chronological, order, although following their time sequence as nearly as is convenient. To attempt any other approach would invite utter confusion. Insofar as a general time sequence appears logical, it is indicated at the head of each chapter.

Most of Carnegie's writings are available to the reader in his books, published miscellaneous works, magazine files, or—principally the speeches—in pamphlet form in larger libraries. Because of the immense volume of his letters and the fact that few have been published, attention to them is here limited to representative examples based on texts reprinted in biographical works.

In regard to the personal origin of his writings, it has not seemed necessary to resort to verbal analyses, since both style and external evidence are clear and convincing. Carnegie wrote to convince, to spread ideas, to influence others. By his own statement he considered his writings more important than even his most outstanding accomplishments in other fields. Perhaps, despite their neglect in the past half century, he was right. His pride would never have allowed him to present the work of a ghost writer as his own. The day of the ghost writer had not yet arrived. As the first great writing industrialist, it was he, more than any other, who created a place for this faceless phantom.

Yet the assumption that Carnegie employed such aides is not surprising; rather it is in keeping with the career of a man whose life was a tissue of contradictions: the boy impoverished by industrialization who used the machine to become one of the world's richest men; the apologist for labor who condoned and perhaps approved one of the greatest crimes against unionization; the flag-waving American whose heart still held tightly to his native Scotland; the man who "must push inordinately" the pursuit of wealth, then used the same energy to give it away. Thus it seems natural, if not poetically just, that the monster he helped to create should have been used to siphon off the one thing in life he valued most: credit for his own ideas.

The author is particularly grateful for the assistance given him by Joseph F. Wall, who provided him with materials from the United States Steel Corporation's Carnegie files, which are no longer open to the public; to Kitty Sullivan Lowder for endless hours of search in Pittsburgh newspaper files; and to the reference staff of Carnegie Library of Pittsburgh, chiefly Marie Zinni and her aides in its Pennsylvania Room. Special thanks are owed to Helene Snyder Smith, the author's coworker, for research, advice, encouragement, ideas, and other assistance without which the book would probably never have been completed.

GEORGE SWETNAM

Chronology

1835   Born at Dunfermline, Scotland, November 25; first of two sons of William Carnegie, unemployed weaver, and his wife, Margaret Morrison.

1843   Enters the Rolland school, near his home. Brother, Tom, born.

1848   Comes to America with parents and brother, settling in Allegheny, now a part of Pittsburgh. First job as a bobbin boy in a cotton mill.

1850   Becomes telegraph messenger.

1851   Becomes telegraph operator. Takes press wire for newspapers.

1853   Operator for Thomas A. Scott, Pennsylvania Railroad division superintendent. Soon his assistant. First published work, letters to the *Pittsburgh Dispatch*.

1855   William Carnegie dies.

1856   Becomes assistant division superintendent. First printed book (probable), *Rules for the Government of The Pennsylvania R. R. Company's Telegraph.*
First investment: $500 for ten shares of Adams Express Co. stock.

1859   Becomes division superintendent of railroad.

1861   Called to Washington to organize telegraph service.

1862   First trip back to Scotland. Silent partner in bridge firm.

1863   Income over $47,000, only $2,400 from railroad.

1865   Leaves railroad. Organizes bridge and iron firms. Goes on walking tour of Europe.

1866   Expands and consolidates industrial holdings.

1867   Moves to New York and comes in contact with cultural influences.

1868   Writes memo planning early retirement and life of culture instead of money-making.

1869   Begins bond sales overseas, totaling $30 million in four years.

1873   Builds Edgar Thomson steel mill largely with money from bond sales.

1878   Trip around the world. *Round the World* printed for private distribution.

1880   Organizes newspaper syndicate in Britain.

1881   Coaching trip in England and Scotland. Gives library to Dunfermline—first of over 2,800 to towns all over the world. Begins organizing chain of liberal newspapers in Britain.

1882   First article published in a major journal, *Fortnightly Review*. *Our Coaching Trip* printed for private distribution.

1883   *Our Coaching Trip* revised and published as *An American Four-in-Hand in Britain*.

1884   *Round the World* revised and published.

1885   Abandons and sells newspaper chain.

1886   *Triumphant Democracy* published. Mother and only brother die within a few days.

1887   Marries Louise Whitfield in New York.

1889   *Wealth* published in *North American Review*.

1891   Writes first draft of *Autobiography*. Carnegie Hall built.

1892   Homestead steel strike. Carnegie bitterly attacked by press.

1893   *Triumphant Democracy* revised and republished.

1896   Gives Carnegie Institute to Pittsburgh.

1897   Daughter Margaret born.

1898   Buys Skibo Castle, in Scotland.

1900   *The Gospel of Wealth* published. Founds Carnegie Trade Schools, later Carnegie Institute of Technology, now Carnegie–Mellon University.

1901   Sells out steel holdings and gives up industry. Founds Carnegie Relief Fund for retiring workers. Makes first Scottish Education grant.

1902   *The Empire of Business* published. Becomes Lord Rector of St. Andrews University. Builds residence at Fifth Avenue and 91st Street, New York. Founds Carnegie Institution in Washington.

Chronology

1903 President of the Iron and Steel Institute. Builds Hague Peace Palace.

1904 Establishes first Hero Fund.

1905 *James Watt* published. Establishes Foundation for the Advancement of Teaching.

1906 Resumes writing and begins revising *Autobiography*.

1907 Visit to Emperor Wilhelm II of Germany.

1908 *Problems of Today* published.

1910 Sets up Endowment for International Peace.

1911 Sets up first Carnegie Corporation for the advancement and diffusion of knowledge.

1912 Last published address.

1914 Leaves Scotland for last time. Abandons *Autobiography*.

1915 Health weakened by respiratory attack.

1916 Last magazine article published, in *Woman's Home Companion*.

1919 Daughter marries Roswell Miller. Dies August 11, at summer home in Massachusetts.

CHAPTER 1

White-Haired Scotch Devil: 1835-1865

EVEN in his teens Andrew Carnegie was a writer, and writing was his greatest outlet. Late in life he recorded that, "Indeed, my early letters to friends in Scotland, when fourteen, are said to be better than those of this date."[1] At eighteen he used his pen for the same purpose as in later life: to spread his ideas and to accomplish his ends.

Writing, like speaking, came to the young immigrant naturally. He was born into a voluble family of Scottish liberals, and wrote just as he talked. As his ability at speaking improved, so did his literary style. Early experiences even determined much of his subject matter. Poverty and wealth, politics, industry, and patriotism were all concerns of his childhood surroundings.

Andrew Carnegie was born on November 25, 1835, in Dunfermline, Scotland, first of the two sons of William and Margaret Morrison Carnegie. A sister died in infancy, and the younger son, Thomas, was his junior by eight years. As an only child Andrew must have been rather spoiled, since he was not required to go to school until he was past eight. Then he attended a one-teacher institution near his home.[2] Perhaps finances may have had something to do with the delay. His father was a weaver—one of many in Scotland's ancient capital who had been thrown out of work by the introduction of the power loom.

Faced with absolute want, the family borrowed money and came to America in 1848, settling near relatives in a poverty-stricken area of Allegheny, Pa., now part of the city of Pittsburgh. Things were little better in the new land. William Carnegie, unable to endure work in a cotton mill for long, picked up a little money weaving and peddling linens. Mrs. Carnegie, obviously the strong member of the family, largely supported them by binding shoes, a trade she had learned from her father when

17

a girl. Andrew had to give up any hope of further schooling and go to work, first at $1.25 a week as a bobbin boy in the cotton mill, shortly afterward at $2 a week tending a small boiler and oil-treating the product in a bobbin factory owned by a friend of the family.

J. F. Wall notes that although Carnegie was aware of what indigence meant, he never fully experienced grinding poverty, as many of his playmates did. His parents, in particular his mother, shielded him from the full impact, and as a result he was "more an observer than a participant." With this early protective environment it became easy to extol the virtues of poverty —one of his favorite themes throughout life.[3]

Immigrants from the British Isles were little if any more popular in Pittsburgh in that "Know Nothing" era than were their successors from Central Europe a generation later. Andrew and a few other young "Scotchies" had to fight their way out of some difficulties, which may have contributed to his later pugnacity and determination to win every contest. It also encouraged his Scottish patriotism, but before long he was becoming strongly American in his sympathies.[4]

I *Would-Be Reporter*

Trusted with the task of doing his employer's small bit of accounting and billing, young Carnegie took night classes in Pittsburgh to learn double-entry bookkeeping. But what he always considered the most important break of his life came early in 1850 when his uncle recommended him for a job as an extra messenger boy for the recently opened telegraph office in Pittsburgh. His small stature made him look even younger than his fourteen years, and he wisely insisted that his father stay outside while he went into the office to apply for the work. He admitted later that he had also thought of the effect of his father's broad Scottish dialect, preferring to trust to his own more Americanized tongue.[5]

The new job paid more money and had many perquisites, including free admission to the town's theaters, where the youth acquired a lifetime devotion to Shakespeare. He worked hard, memorizing the locations of all the city's business houses and learning to recognize the faces of its prominent men, many of whom came to know him. Since Pittsburgh then had a population of somewhat over 46,000 and Allegheny almost half that number,[6] this represented considerable effort. He also gave strict attention to the telegraph instruments, and in a little more than a year was promoted to a position as operator.

One of the sixteen-year-old operator's duties was to take the press wire and make copies for the reporters of the five newspapers which subscribed to the service. The contact gave him a feeling of importance and a desire to become a newspaperman— a yearning that was to persist for more than thirty years, until bitter experience convinced him that there were some battles even he could not win.

Meanwhile, as he labored with key, sounder, and pad, he was offered a position as personal operator to Thomas A. Scott, Pittsburgh Division superintendent of the Pennsylvania Railroad, which had been opened for through service between Philadelphia and Pittsburgh just a year earlier. Regular train dispatching by telegraph was still in the future when the appointment was made on February 1, 1853, but the railroad had enough business to need its own line. Though a youth of barely seventeen may seem a strange choice for the position, Scott was a good judge of men. And besides, Andy was reputed to be only the third operator in America who had learned to take messages by sound, discarding the clumsy tape rolls designed by Morse to record messages until the dots and dashes could be translated into letters.

Always a voracious reader, young Carnegie had been using a library of some 400 books which Col. James Anderson of Allegheny had set up, and later enlarged.[7] Anderson, a retired manufacturer, had allowed working boys to use the library free, taking out one book a week. But after it was turned over to the city, a new librarian interpreted this as applying only to bound apprentices, and demanded that Carnegie pay a fee of $2 a year. Small though the fee might be, it was still an important amount to Carnegie and many of his friends who were affected by the ruling. On May 9, 1853, he took up the cudgels in a letter to the *Pittsburgh Dispatch*, probably published through the good offices of a reporter friend. "Mr. Editor," he wrote. "Believing that you take a deep interest in whatever tends to elevate, instruct and improve the youth of this country, I am induced to call your attention to the following."[8] After citing the principal facts of the situation, he continued: "Every working boy has been freely admitted only requiring his parents or guardian to become surety. But its means of doing good have been greatly circumscribed by new directors who refuse to allow any boy *who is not learning a trade* and *bound* for a stated time to become a member. I rather think that the new directors have misunderstood the generous donor's *intentions*. It can hardly be thought that he meant to exclude boys employed in stores merely because they are not bound."

Young Carnegie signed the communication "A Working Boy though not bound," and the reference to store workers may have been intended to conceal his identity. After all, a dispute over $2 a year might be thought beneath a telegraph operator making $35 a month.

The letter was printed four days later, and on May 16 a reply appeared, signed X.Y.Z., criticizing it, and stating that for a time others than apprentices had been admitted free, "but for reasons it became absolutely necessary to admit none but those for whose benefit the donation was made." Next day Carnegie replied with a letter which argued; "The question is, was the donation intended for use of apprentices only in strict meaning of the word, viz. persons learning a trade and *bound,* or whether it was designed for working boys whether bound or not? If the former be correct then the managers have certainly misunderstood the generous donor's intentions—[*sic*]."

Three days later appeared a notice in the *Dispatch*: "A 'Working Boy' will confer a favor by calling at our office." There the librarian quietly agreed to make the concessions demanded. The success so elated the young railroader that he was certain he wanted to become a reporter. For years afterward, in speeches to news groups and in conversation with newspapermen, he would often confide: "The only reason I am not one of you is because no Pittsburgh paper in those days would give me a job."

II *Writing Railroader*

Lacking such an offer—if he really had not already made up his mind in regard to a change—young Carnegie continued as operator and soon as assistant to Scott in the railroad office. But his work never interfered with his continuing to write for publication. At first there were more letters to the *Dispatch,* then to the *Pittsburgh Commercial Journal,* and on May 12, 1854, to Horace Greeley's *New York Tribune*—printed under Carnegie's name.

Writing letters to newspapers was a custom he did not give up until his health broke when he was almost eighty. During the last twenty years of his active life, 177 letters from Andrew Carnegie were printed in such journals as the *New York Times, Tribune,* and *World*; London *Times*; *Manufacturer's Record*; and *Iron Trade Review.*[9]

Carnegie was never a devotee of formal religion, but at this period he was attending the Church of the New Jerusalem (Swedenborgian) in Allegheny with his family, taking part in its Sunday School and singing in the choir. A year after the "working boy" incident he was writing to a church periodical, *Dewdrop,* commending its stand against all war in terms that anticipate his peace efforts half a century later. His letters to his relatives in Scotland at this period foreshadow the super-patriotism that was to ripen in thirty more years into *Triumphant Democracy.* In an 1853 letter to his cousin George Lauder, Jr., he states the main thesis of that work pretty clearly: "But you may reply, Government has little or nothing to do with the state of affairs. Why then, I would ask, the contrast between the U. States and the Canadas? They were settled by the same people, at the same time, under the same Government—and look at the difference! Where are her Railroads, Telegraphs and Canals? her . . . potent Press? We have given to the world a Washington . . . —Ah, Dod,[10] what has Canada ever produced?"[11]

It was about this period that young Carnegie again demonstrated the courage and the executive ability that were to characterize his later life in such a high degree. Only a short time after he had begun working for the railroad, he arrived at the office one morning to discover that there had been a

serious accident which had halted all traffic, except that the
eastbound express was creeping along from station to station,
a flagman signaling its progress at every curve. Knowing that
nothing else could move without direct orders from the superintendent, who might not arrive for some time, the youthful
operator ascertained the position of each train, issued orders
under Scott's name, and soon had everything in order.

When Scott arrived at the office some two hours later, the
youth explained the situation and handed him the stack of
telegrams, not sure whether his temerity might bring instant
discharge. The superintendent didn't say a word, but a few
days later Carnegie learned that his employer had confided to
an associate:

"Do you know what that little white-haired Scotch devil of mine
did today? . . . I'm damned if he didn't run every train on the division
in my name, without the slightest authority."
"And did he do it all right?"
"Oh, yes, all right!"[12]

Carnegie's father died in 1855, and a year later Scott was
transferred to Altoona, Pa., his young assistant and the family
going along. It was at this time that the railroad began operating
all trains on telegraphic orders, and there can be little doubt
that Carnegie wrote the rule book for telegraphers, of which
an 1863 issue was in the files of the railroad at Pittsburgh.[13]

Certain phrases not ordinarily used in Pennsylvania at the
time, such as "tea" for the evening meal,[14] make it almost certain
that one of the Scottish contingent Carnegie had assembled for
the railroad is the author. And despite the printed statement
that it was Robert Pitcairn—then in the General Superintendent's
office—who inaugurated telegraphic train operation for the road,[15]
no one familiar with Carnegie's style could doubt that he was
the author. Certainly it could not have been Pitcairn, the only
other Scottish operator then in a position to compile such a rule
book. No one who has read any of his writings—full of confusion and with interminable sentences of piled-up, loosely
linked phrases—could possibly believe he could have produced
its terse, forceful style.[16] Another Scot, David McCargo, was in

position to have written the book by 1859,[17] but it seems incredible that the railroad would have operated for three years without such a set of rules. If the objection be raised that Carnegie fails to mention it in his *Autobiography*—the same thing is true of several of his more important works.[18]

Early in 1859 Scott was again promoted, and the twenty-three-year-old Carnegie was made superintendent of the Pittsburgh Division, returning to the city to make his home. No longer did the family live in the flats of Allegheny, however. Carnegie and his mother secured a house in Homewood, an eastern suburb of the city, sparsely settled up to that time, but near the railroad. The choice was a fortunate one, for the house they chose was in a small pocket of education and culture. As always, Andy's charm and wit gained him a ready entrance into the group, where he was able to gain a better appreciation of music, and expand his knowledge, which had been largely limited to the English and Scottish classics. In this atmosphere, also, he found occasion to polish his formerly awkward manners, and improve his grammar and speaking ability.

While still in Altoona he had borrowed money to invest in the Woodruff sleeping car, which was an immediate success, giving him his first substantial income from stocks. Soon after Drake's discovery of oil in the Allegheny valley, Carnegie and some friends leased a farm there, which brought them a fantastic return not long afterwards.

With the beginning of the Civil War, his former chief called him to Washington to organize the telegraph service, Scott himself being head of railroad transportation. Carnegie was only there for a few months, however, and soon was able to spend most of his time back in Pittsburgh again, investing and making money. He was present at the first battle of Bull Run, managing a telegraph office, and became so much interested in sending a press story on how the Union army was winning, that he barely escaped being captured by Confederate forces. Never able to tolerate high temperatures well, he suffered a heat stroke soon afterward from which he was long in recovering. In an effort to regain his health he and his mother took a trip to Scotland in the summer of 1862.

On his return he plunged again into business with such

success that a memo he made of his 1863 income discloses that it totaled nearly $48,000, of which his railroad salary provided only $2,400. For the remainder of the war period, it appears, the young industrialist gave virtually all his time to investment, with great success.

CHAPTER 2

Young Man of Affairs: 1865-1886

FOR a man who amassed one of the great fortunes of his era, and whose principal reputation is based on industry, Andrew Carnegie was surprisingly casual about most business matters.

May of 1865 would have seemed a most unlikely time for him to take an extended vacation. George Pullman was beginning to threaten Central Transportation Co., the sleeping car firm Carnegie had formed with Woodruff.[1] He had just enlarged and reorganized Piper and Shiffler Co. into his Keystone Bridge Works a month earlier.[2] And in March he had merged his five-month-old Cyclops Iron Co.—his first venture into basic metal production—with a rival firm, as the Union Iron Mills.[3] Yet without the slightest apparent hesitation he left these and his numerous other business affairs in the hands of his twenty-two-year-old brother, Tom, and sailed off with two companions for a nine-month tour of Europe. The obvious explanation appears to be that Carnegie had already decided something he would put on paper three years later: that his most important business was not to make money, but to acquire culture and be of influence in the world.

I The Quest for Culture

Since his return from Scotland in 1862—to some extent even earlier[4]—Andrew had studied with tutors, making up for the education he had missed because of having to work hard in childhood. Just as he had studied hard at double-entry bookkeeping in night classes at thirteen, he labored at French and cultural subjects after returning from Altoona to Pittsburgh as a railroad divisional superintendent at twenty-four. He had been inspired by Rebecca Stewart, Scott's sister-in-law, who came to Altoona to care for his children after his wife's death.

25

But a stronger force was the society in which he found himself after returning to Pittsburgh.

There after a few months he bought his mother a house in the small, new, residential suburb of Homewood. It had taken its name from the mansion of William Wilkins, a former judge, cabinet member, and ambassador to Russia, an elder statesman and dean of the Pittsburgh bar. Eager young Andy found himself welcomed at the Wilkins home and that of William Coleman, a well-known businessman, later Tom Carnegie's father-in-law. But he gave principal credit to another neighbor, Leila Addison. Miss Addison was the daughter of a physician and granddaughter of a judge, both deceased, and lived in Homewood with her widowed mother. Mrs. Addison was a native of Edinburgh, and had reportedly been tutored by Thomas Carlyle.

Up to that time Andy had been a brash, well-read but intentionally rugged and very successful young man. Meeting with the Addisons he suddenly glimpsed the gulf between him and the world of real culture. He felt that it was "the wee drap o' Scotch bluid atween us" which aroused their interest in his welfare.

"Miss Addison became an ideal friend because she undertook to improve the rough diamond, if it were indeed a diamond at all," Carnegie later wrote.[5] "She was my friend, because my severest critic. I began to pay strict attention to my language, and to the English classics . . . also to note how much better it was to be gentle in tone and manner, polite and courteous to all—in short, better behaved."

By the time of the 1865 trip to Europe this training had borne fruit. Although still far from the polished, urbane man he would become, Carnegie was able to converse in understandable—if somewhat gapped—French, and to make the most of the cultural opportunities which the tour afforded. If he failed in full appreciation of scenic wonders,[6] it was not so much from ignorance as from his interests, which always ran much more to people than to things.

Carnegie sailed from New York in mid-May, along with two boyhood friends, Henry Phipps (a partner in his iron venture) and John Vandevort. They stayed in Britain until September, and even after they had gone to the Continent, Carnegie passed up the trip to Switzerland in order to improve his French in Paris, and return briefly to London to secure the rights on a new process for making rails.

II   *Correspondent for the* Commercial

Young Carnegie had been greatly impressed by Bayard Taylor's *Views A-Foot,* which came out in 1847 and had been read and discussed by the group at Homewood.[7] Taylor, just twenty-one years earlier, had gone overseas as an almost penniless young apprentice printer, financing two years in Europe on $500 made by writing for newspapers.[8] Carnegie, though far from penniless, and estimating the cost of his jaunt at $3,000,[9] planned to emulate his idol by writing letters to the Pittsburgh newspapers. A careful check of all available newspaper files for his period abroad, however, discloses only two published letters, both in the *Commercial.* It is likely that not more than three were written, as he explained in letters to his family and friends that he would like to write more, but found himself too busy making the most of his opportunities to see, learn, and enjoy the trip.[10] The third letter may have been declined by the newspaper's editor, C. D. Brigham, because of its controversial content. On September 29 Carnegie wrote from Paris to the Pittsburgh printer and news-dealer W. S. Haven that he had received the paper "and have occupied myself giving my views on Protection, a subject Mr. Brigham is stirring up thoroughly and well. . . . Mr. Brigham, I suppose, will give my protection letter his care. It isn't the Pittsburgh doctrine, I know, but it will do good in stirring up the subject. I have had it hot and heavy with the English, but that Carisbrooke Castle illustration I have always found effective."[11] Carnegie's reference makes it appear probable that he wrote and sent the article, but apparently its sentiments were so far from the "Pittsburgh doctrine" that Brigham failed to print it.

Whatever may have been Carnegie's sentiments in regard to Bayard Taylor's work, none of the three subjects chosen for his letters show any indication of copying Taylor's style or subject matter.

The first—dated at Inverness, Scotland, August 21, and printed in the *Commercial* on September 21—deals with fish breeding, and opens with a disclaimer of any intention to write the usual type of travel letter:

Descriptive letters from abroad are now-a-days so readily prepared from the omnipresent guide books, whch give not only dates and particulars, but pages, written in excellent style, upon the memories and associations which a visit calls forth, that one feels a laudable disinclination to seek such publicity as your columns would afford, for what the guide would mostly be entitled to the credit of. But what we saw yesterday is so utterly foreign to the domain of the professional *litterateur* that we are prompted to write you in regard to it, in the hope that the subject may receive some attention at home.

Carnegie then proceeds to give a careful and accurate report of a salmon hatchery near Perth, including the method of gathering and fertilizing the eggs, dimensions of the ponds, costs of labor and materials, and the results. The most impressive of these results (and italicized by the ever profit-conscious writer) was that the fishing privileges on the Tay returned "*thirty-five thousand dollars* in gold every season, over and above former rentals." The investment was "not exceeding $2,500, and maintained for not exceeding $1,000 per annum," to produce 300,000 salmon every other year weighing seven pounds each in four to six months.

Proving that he would have become a good newspaperman if he had gone into that field as a young man, Carnegie bore in mind that a regional paper would be interested in the story's local angles: "There are certainly many streams, throughout the United States, formerly noted for a bountiful supply of various kinds of fish which have become scarce, and which could readily be restored, at a trifling expense. Who will be the first to move in this matter, and thus add to the resources of our sacred land?"

Using the names of various Pittsburgh friends who shared his passion for fishing, he continued:

For the sake of John Hampton, Perry Knox, Tom Scott, David Book, Geo. Findley, and sundry other friends, ardent disciples of old Izaak's, and not without a slight degree of personal interest in the premises, we made particular inquiries as to whether the coveted brook trout could be multiplied in similar manner, and was assured that there was not the shadow of a doubt about it. Oh! Shades of Tub Mill, Big Ben creek, Kittanning Point and Bell's Mills! how you grow upon me. We will have committees formed at once, subscriptions raised, and fill you full of "bonnie trout." There will be no such thing as empty baskets any more, even for Judge ————. No longer will we condescend to use the worm, but the speckled beauties so numerous, so large, so gay, will continually, "rise to the fly. . . ."

[We] set ourselves thinking . . . what he should be called who caused twenty salmon to spring up where one existed, if he who made two blades of grass grow where one flourished before were justly called a benefactor.[12]

Perhaps because of the apparent rebuff on his tariff article, Carnegie sent nothing more to the *Commercial* on political and economic matters, although we know from his later writings that these were among his principal interests. Always the pragmatist, and with little time for such correspondence, he would limit his effort to something which gave more promise of results.

His third and apparently final letter to the *Commercial* is dated from Amsterdam, November 15, although he was in Berlin before that time, and had planned to leave Holland around November 7.[13] It appeared in the *Commercial* on December 13, like its predecessor under the heading "Our Foreign Correspondence," taking up the same space, a full column. Like the earlier letter it was signed only with the initials, "A.C."

Once more Carnegie begins his letter by demonstrating that its contents are newsworthy:

Ask twenty Americans who have made the "Grand Tour," and a majority of them will confess that they omitted to visit Holland, while nineteen out of the twenty will never have seen the northern portion of it. It is even doubtful whether a Pittsburgher ever trod the dykes at the Helder unless James Park Jr. extended his travels thus far when "doing" Europe twenty years ago. And yet there is no country under the sun where a traveler meets with such strange sights as in the region indicated. Nor is there one which will more amply repay tourists for the time necessary for an excursion through it.

The article makes scarcely any mention of Amsterdam itself, and none at all of the city's foreign trade, cultural institutions, and botanical and zoological gardens—subjects which certainly must have drawn Carnegie's interest. Instead, he devotes the whole article to the dykes and reclamation of land from the sea. He launches his discourse in most interesting fashion: "To all other places the fates have at least vouchsafed dry land ready prepared for occupation, and all that was requisite was to locate and begin the cultivation of the soil in the preparation of which they had taken no part, but to the unfortunate Dutchman nature seems to have distributed no favors. The alluvium from the Rhine and other rivers flowing into the North Sea, mixed with such mud as that ocean might throw upon the shoals when agitated by storms, was all that he received."

The description of the dykes is more pictorial than the technical style that might be expected of Carnegie, He lays out in steps the work that was necessary to reclaim the land—dyke-building, then pumping out the water:

After the Hollander had completed the dykes, he was called upon to begin the second part of the work, which consisted in pumping by windmills, out of the inclosure made, the water which had accumulated from the last raids of the ocean, and for this purpose he put nine thousand windmills to work, many of them being of immense size, the arms frequently exceeding one hundred feet in length. The monotony of the scenery is greatly relieved by these mills, which abound everywhere. From the top of one in Rotterdam we counted fifty-two, all busily at work.

Evidently Carnegie had by this time discovered Cervantes, even if he had not perfected his own syntax: "Coming up the Maas by boat in a beautiful moonlit night, they seemed to us like a squadron of giants combatting imaginary foes, as they cast their weird-like arms about, and displayed so much activity while all around slumbered."

After a concise but comparatively complete discussion of the dangers—"At one time an inundation . . . drowned eighty thousand persons. . . . At another period it is stated that one hundred thousand persons were cut off. . . . These were ocean's victims.

The losses by internal floods have been equally severe."— Carnegie uses the courage of the Dutch as a text in chiding faint-hearted Americans:

It may tend to reassure some of our timid citizens at home, who shudder at the expense of our national debt, to know that competent authority has estimated the cost of the Hydraulic Works of the Dutch, all of which are unnecessary in our favored land, at one and a half thousand million dollars (gold). If to this can be added the annual cost of maintenance, we have a total not far from equal to our entire indebtedness, all sunk and settled for by three and a half millions of Dutchmen. What cannot America do with its ever-increasing population and its manifold resources?

Although not much given to efforts at humor in writing—although fond of jokes in real life—Carnegie does become playful in discussing the problem of building on unstable land, where piles had to be sunk more than a hundred feet to support foundations for the houses. Then turning serious, he discusses the courageous fight of the Dutch to maintain their independence, showing some feeling in the account of how twice in history they had opened the dykes to repel invaders. He adds, half serious, half tongue-in-cheek: "No country has so secure a defense as Holland. Other nations may continue to spend millions on fortifications, and throw away, before they are used, the implements which have cost so much, only to replace them with others which the march of events, or the progress of military science, shall in turn render useless. He aspires not to be ironclad, but why should he, when nature has made him waterproof!"

The letters are not great literature, but they are interesting as examples of Carnegie's early style and thought. It is regrettable that his letter on the tariff question was wasted. It would be interesting to compare it, for style as well as ideas, with his later writings on the subject. Slight as they are, the letters give some opportunity to observe changes in his style and thought before the beginning of his truly serious writing, more than a decade later. Except in depth of treatment, they do not greatly differ from similar descriptive matter in his family letters. But these, of course, were largely taken up with personal references and discussions of business affairs. One passage from a letter written while still on board ship, outward bound, reveals his intent and suggests how far ahead his planning sometimes ran: "An ocean voyage is good fun, and I think we might do as the Duncans do (They are on board)—have a summer estate in Scotland and go over every summer as they do to enjoy it. How does the idea strike the two members of the Carnegie firm at Homewood? Will Pittencrief, or Pittrearie, answer? . . . It would suit me exactly."[14]

Although Carnegie made no more walking tours, there was seldom a summer in his life from that time on which he failed to spend in Scotland, England, or on the Continent. He sometimes took his mother along, although they had a summer home at Cresson, in the mountains of Pennsylvania. And following his marriage in 1887, he and his wife spent every summer in Scotland until the war clouds of 1914 made it impossible. In 1902 he did buy Pittencrief, making it a park for his home town.

III *A Bachelor in New York*

Carnegie returned from his walking trip in the early spring of 1868, and threw himself into business affairs with renewed vigor. But as his world had expanded, Pittsburgh had become too small for either his interests or his desires. Late in the autumn of 1867[15] he opened an office in New York. His mother went with him, and they lived in the city's finest hotel, the St. Nicholas, leaving the house at Homewood to Tom, who had recently married the daughter of a Carnegie partner.

The move was a fortunate one. New York was not only the center of American business, but of culture as well. Here Carnegie was able to attend theaters, art galleries, opera, and other important events, and to engage the best of tutors for studies he felt he still needed. He studied literature, history, philosophy, and economics, but found languages difficult.

Money was still rolling in. Not only were his steel works and other investments successful, but he had come to be trusted by the leading European bankers, and made a handsome commission in selling over $30 million in bonds to them during the next five years.[16]

Both in the mountains and in the city, one of his favorite pastimes was riding horseback. In New York he was—as a young, well-spoken millionaire—one of the most eligible bachelors. His riding companions in Central Park were among the cream of society, and his mother often invited groups of them as guests in summer, providing rooms at the Mountain House, Cresson's best hotel.[17] He may have caused many hearts to beat fast, but there was no serious romance in his life until he was almost fifty.

IV *Proto "Gospel of Wealth"*

Not much more than a year after moving to New York to live, Carnegie sat down at year's end to take stock. The result is a singular memorandum not known until it was found among his papers more than half a century later, after his death, attached to a brief listing of "Income for 1868." Headed "dec^r 68, St. Nicholas Hotel, New York," it reads:

Thirty three and an income of 50,000$ per annum.

By this time two years I can arrange all my business as to secure at least 50,000$ per annum—Beyond this never earn—make no effort to increase fortune but spend the surplus each year for benevolent purposes. Cast aside business forever, except for others.

Settle in Oxford & get a thorough education making the acquaintance of literary men. This will take three years active work—pay especial attention to speaking in public. Settle then in London & purchase a controlling interest in some newspaper or live review & give the general management of it attention, taking a part in public matters, especially those connected with education & improvement of the poorer classes—

Man must have an idol—the amassing of wealth is one of the worst species of idolatry—no idol more debasing than the worship of money—Whatever I engage in I must push inordinately, therefore should I be careful to choose that life which will be the most elevating in its character—To continue much longer overwhelmed by business cares and with most of my thoughts wholly upon the way to make money in the shortest time must degrade me beyond hope of permanent recovery.

I will resign business at thirty five, but during the ensuing two

years I wish to spend the afternoons in receiving instruction, and in
reading systematically.[18]

Much of that plan did work out, but not so soon nor so
easily as Carnegie had anticipated. The end of two years found
him still rich, but locked in a financial and industrial fight
to the death. Like the hunter who was sent up the tree to catch
a bear, he had to learn in the hard school of experience how to
turn loose of the bear of business. Thirty years later he thought
he had reached his objective, only to have the sale of his
interests break down. It was almost exactly thirty-two years
after the writing of the memorandum that Carnegie gained his
retirement objective.

For all that, he was but partly turned aside from his purpose.
He made the most of every opportunity for education and influence, until he became one of the best-known men of his era.
The brash young steel-maker and bond salesman seemed to
gravitate towards important and interesting people, and they
toward him. Just as he had quickly come to know and be known
by the principal men of Pittsburgh when he was a messenger
boy and then a railroader, he somehow found ways of getting
to know the people in New York—not just the rich, but the
intelligent and cultured. Unlike most Pittsburgh millionaires
and other new rich, Carnegie made no effort to court the favor
of Mrs. Astor or become one of the Four Hundred,[19] and had no
hesitation in expressing his disdain for the plutocrat.[20]

V *Pursuit of Culture*

His most fortunate contact after moving to the big city was
becoming acquainted with Courtlandt Palmer through a mutual
interest in technical—as opposed to classical—education.[21] Carnegie, who often commented on the importance of chance hap-
penings, noted in his *Autobiography*[22] that for a while, until
new friendships were made, he and his mother were emotionally
and by mutual interest largely dependent on Pittsburgh.

"The literary life of New York was a sort of Dutch-English
family party as late as the beginning of the nineties,"[23] and
Palmer, the son of a rich merchant, was prominent in intellectual

circles. Shortly before Carnegie's arrival he had organized the Nineteenth Century Club, which met in his home in Gramercy Park until its growth required larger quarters. At first a discussion group, it later included the reading of assigned papers, in which Carnegie took part. There Carnegie met a stimulating assemblage of people of widely varying opinions, for although Palmer inclined to Positivism his guests included those of all attitudes.

At Palmer's club meetings and less formal gatherings, Carnegie could discuss economics, politics, religion, and literature with many of America's leading thinkers of the day. Among them he met such writers as Moncure D. Conway, George Washington Cable, and Thomas Wentworth Higginson; educators such as Thomas Davidson and Horace Porter; public figures like Abram S. Hewitt, son-in-law of Peter Cooper and later Mayor of New York; statesmen such as Theodore Roosevelt and journalists like John Swinton, chief of the *New York Times* editorial staff. Here were Jewish rabbis, Catholic priests and bishops, Unitarian clergymen, Protestant ministers, and freethinkers such as the great Robert G. Ingersoll. In such company he gained a much wider view of the world than had been available in Pittsburgh. Here he came into contact with the work of Comte, Darwin, and Herbert Spencer,[24] with the latter of whom he formed a warm and enduring friendship. Through acquaintance thus made, Carnegie also came in contact with many of the principal minds of Britain, among them John Morley, who influenced him and was in turn influenced.

One of the most important benefits of Carnegie's friendship with Palmer was being introduced in 1871 to Anne C. L. Botta, for many years the unquestioned queen bee of the New York intelligentsia. Born in 1815 as Anne Lynch, Mrs. Botta was in her mid-fifties at the time they met, already white-haired, always dressed in black, a poet, "author, sculptor, critic, and not least the charming woman of the world."[25] At the time of her death twenty years later Carnegie recalled how they met: "One of her chief characteristics was that of recognizing unknown men and women, and giving them opportunities to benefit, not only from her own stores of wisdom, and from her charming manners and conversation, but from the remarkable class she drew around her. . . . The position of the Bottas enabled them to bring together not only the best people of this country, but to a degree greater than any, so far as I know, the most distinguished visitors from abroad, beyond the ranks of mere title or fashion."[26]

He had been brought to her home by Palmer, and years afterward she told him that he had been invited to return because "some words I had spoken the first night struck her as a genuine note, though unusual."[27] Carnegie rightly considered her home the nearest "in the modern era" to a real salon. "Millionaires and fashionables," he wrote, "are poor substitutes for a cultivated society. Madame Botta's lions could all roar, more or less; they were not compelled to chatter, or be dumb."[28]

As a young poet in her early thirties, Anne Lynch had been praised by Edgar Allan Poe, who was a regular visitor at her Saturday evening soirees, as were many of his friends. "All the lights of contemporary letters brightened these gatherings," notes Hendrick. They included N. P. Willis, Lydia Sigourney, Fitz-Greene Halleck, Daniel Webster, and Henry Clay on their New York visits, and many others. Following Anne's marriage to Vincenzo Botta, professor of Italian literature at New York University, the salons were continued in their home on Murray Hill. During his years of attendance at such functions Carnegie could have met there William Cullen Bryant, Ralph Waldo Emerson, George Ripley, Charles A. Dana, Bronson Alcott, John Bigelow, Henry Ward Beecher, E. C. Stedman, Andrew D. White, Richard Watson Gilder, Julia Ward Howe, Charles Dudley Warner, and scores of other personages of the day, including his early idol, Bayard Taylor. Many of them he certainly did meet, and with some, such as White and Gilder, he formed close friendships.[29]

Distinguished foreigners were also among the visitors at the Botta home, including Charles Kingsley, Justin McCarthy, James A. Froude, and Matthew Arnold. In bringing Arnold to the Botta home in 1883, Carnegie was repaying part of his debt. He had met the poet in England at a party given by Mrs. Henry Yates Thompson, who was one of the great hostesses of Britain, and whose husband owned the *Pall Mall Gazette*, edited by

Morley. When Arnold came to America that October for a lecture tour of 100 appearances, he was Carnegie's guest. His brother, Edwin, also became a close friend of the industrialist.

Now a polished man of the world, Carnegie had no reason to kowtow to anyone, however important. Nor is there any evidence that even in his salad days he had ever met anyone except on a frank and equal basis. Not even his mentor, Herbert Spencer, found himself treated by Carnegie as anything other than an equal. An incident mentioned by both Carnegie and Spencer in their autobiographies is detailed by Hendrick:

At the end of a particular dinner the waiter proffered cheese. Spencer gazed at it unsympathetically, and angrily pushed it aside. "Cheddar! Cheddar!" he shouted in tones so loud that they carried over the dining room. "I said Cheddar, not Cheshire! Bring me Cheddar"—and his fist came down upon the table.

The three companions then began talking about their meetings with well known men. Did they appear as great in the flesh as in their books and public careers? Carnegie insisted that such meetings were usually disappointing; distinguished characters turned out to be so different from the previously formed conception. Mr. Spencer evidently sniffed a personal reference.

"In my case, for example," he asked, "was that so?"

"You more than anybody," replied Carnegie. "I had imagined you, the great philosopher brooding over all things. Never did I dream you could become so excited over the question of Cheddar and Cheshire cheese."[30]

The incident did nothing to interfere with their friendship, and Carnegie commented on it that "Spencer liked stories and was a good laugher."[31] Nor did the incident appear to lessen the philosopher's influence on Carnegie's thinking—at least for some time.

CHAPTER 3

Travel Writer: 1878-1884

DESPITE the fact that Bayard Taylor's *Views A-Foot* had
been one of Carnegie's early inspirations,[1] the commercial
publication of his own two books of travel came to the steel-
maker almost as an accident. Reaction to the newspaper articles
written during his ramble over Europe had apparently been
minimal, except for the pats on the back that friends give anyone
whose work unexpectedly appears in print. Carnegie and his
friends largely gave up their original idea of a walking trip,
using public transportation most of the time. Because of this,
the chatty approach to his subject appeared only in a brief portion of the first printed letter. As a result, Carnegie stumbled
into what was to become the more modern style in travel
writing, although there is no evidence that he ever realized
what he had done.

Both of Carnegie's travel books, in their original form, were
written and published for private distribution to friends, partly
to serve as a "thank you" for their loyal service in staying
at work while he played.[2] Eventually this pattern of devotion
would become such a part of his normal course of life that
he no longer paid it any heed. But up to the spring of his forty-
seventh year, the feeling of gratitude remained strong.[3]

The works which first brought Carnegie to public notice as a
commercially published writer of books were—like the letters to
the *Pittsburgh Commercial* in 1865—accounts of extended tours,
one around the world in 1878, the other a coaching trip for
almost the entire length of England and Scotland three years
later. Internal evidence would indicate that *Round the World*
was written (or largely written) as the trip progressed, while
Carnegie's *Autobiography* specifically states that *Our Coaching
Trip* resulted from brief notes, later amplified.[4] Both were

38

privately printed soon after their composition, and apparently both by Charles Scribner's Sons.[5] A copy of the later volume having come to the notice of Charles Scribner himself, he suggested it might be of interest to the public. With considerable revision, it was published commercially in 1883, and met with enough success that the earlier work was also revised and brought out the following year by the same firm.

In writing the two books, Carnegie harked back for method to Taylor, whom he had probably come to know well during the decade and more since the transfer from Pittsburgh to New York. They moved in the same cultural and literary circles, and could hardly have failed to become friends.[6] The day-by-day diary style of *Views A-Foot* had been for a century the common way of writing a personal account of travel, and even as a boy, young Carnegie must often have noted it in his voluminous reading. He also followed Taylor in using the first person, although to a notably lesser degree, and with far less intrusion of his own tastes and preferences. The principal differences lie in their choice of materials. Taylor spends much more time in describing scenes, especially landscapes, while Carnegie's principal interests are in people and their doings. Taylor views the present scene for itself alone, while Carnegie continually digs into reasons and background, especially history, which Taylor almost completely ignores. Taylor interlards his pages with original poems, while Carnegie constantly inserts quotations—mostly poetry—from his favorite authors, including Shakespeare, Milton, Burns, Scott, and Sir Edwin Arnold, a close friend whose work he much admired. Taylor evidences little interest in economics, politics, and religion, deep concerns which Carnegie constantly introduces into his travel writing.

I Round the World

In its original form, *Round the World* is a purely personal account of a trip taken for pleasure and education. Carnegie wrote it as he went, day by day, with the evident intention from the beginning of publishing it immediately on his return for private distribution to his many friends, too numerous for individual correspondence. Reaching New York on June 24, 1879, he wrote the two final paragraphs at Cresson the following day.[7] The dedication to Tom Carnegie, dated "Braemar Cottage, Cresson, July, 1879," reads: "To my brother, and trusty associates, who toiled at home that I might spend abroad, these notes are affectionately inscribed by the grateful author." Young as he was—not yet forty-three—Carnegie already felt a parental relationship with his partners and employees, which apparently squared with their own feelings toward him.

Long devoted to newspapers, Carnegie had learned to copy their slam-bang style, and leaped head-first into his story:

New York, Saturday, Oct. 12, 1878.
Bang! click! the desk closes, the key turns, and good-by for a year[8] to my wards—that goodly cluster over which I have watched with parental solicitude for many a day; their several cribs, full of records and labelled Union Iron Mills, Lucy Furnaces ... but for the present I bid them farewell; I'm off for a holiday, and the rise and fall of iron and steel "affecteth me not."

He immediately recalls his former long vacation, the walking trip through Europe, and how at its end he and two companions had pledged themselves to take another which would extend all around the globe: "Years ago, Vandy, Harry, and I, standing in the crater of Mount Vesuvius ... resolved that some day, instead of turning back as we had then to do, we would make a tour round the Ball."[9]

For the "long weary hours" of the Pacific voyage he turned to literature. His mother had sent him a set of Shakespeare "in thirteen handy volumes," and that would do. But immediately he must explain to Robert Burns that the Scot is not being neglected: "No, no Robin, no need of taking you in my trunk; I have you in my heart from 'Tam O'Shanter' to the 'Daisy.'"

Five of the next six sections (each headed by the date) open in the explosive newspaper style of the day: "What is this? a telegram!" "All aboard for 'Frisco!'" "Desolation! In the great desert!" "A palace, truly!" "At last!" But from this point the technique is used only at the approach to land, and very rarely in the remainder of the book. For the most part, after the first dozen pages the sections open smoothly—most often with indications of progress in the trip, but about a third of the time with discussions of places or events.

Perhaps partly in relation to his time for writing, Carnegie alloted his space on a fairly even basis of time spent, with certain exceptions. The number of pages (229) is nearly the same as the number of days (243). But the cutting down sharply on the coverage of the approximately 100 days spent on long rail trips or sea voyages, he was able to give from two to two-and-one-half pages a day to the time spent in visiting Oriental lands. In making these reductions, he allowed less than one page for each day which elapsed from his leaving the office to landing in Japan. To the six weeks from his leaving Alexandria to arrival at Cresson, he gave only twenty-two pages. This was apparently due not to failure in keeping his diary, but rather to concern for keeping the book's length within bounds. In his *Autobiography* Carnegie quotes two "illustrations from our 'Round the World' trip," one of about 100, the other of 150 words. The first is from the time spent at Singapore, and the second details a visit to a camp of Laplanders "on the way to the North Cape" of Norway, within the Arctic Circle.[10] Singularly, neither appears in the published versions of the book.

There is a noteworthy progression in outlook as Carnegie proceeds with the journey and the writing. His style is always intensely personal (although avoiding the use of "I" and the intrusion of individual tastes so common in Taylor's *Views A-Foot*), but the personal view becomes increasingly public in its concerns. Where he reports arguments with persons he meets in his travels, Carnegie usually offers a fair assessment from his point of view (a characteristic of all his writing), even when the discussion doesn't go his way. For example, he presents a colloquy with a Parsee over the disposal of the dead:

Parsees cannot burn the dead, because fire should not be prostituted to so vile a use. They cannot bury, because the earth should not be desecrated with the dead, neither should the sea; and therefore God has provided vultures, which cannot be defiled, to absorb the flesh of the dead. I said to him that the mere thought of violence

offered to our dead caused us to shudder. "Then what do you think
of worms?" he asked. This was certainly an effective estoppel. "It
comes to this," he continued, "a question of birds or worms."
"You are right," (I had to admit it) I said; "after all, it's not worth
disputing about."[11]

Carnegie very seldom attempts humor in any of his writing.
One of the evidences that he did not contemplate commercial
publication when he first wrote is his occasionally becoming
playful in the original version of *Round the World*. Most of
these instances occur near the beginning, largely when he is
on a train or the ship, with little else to write about, it would
seem. He tries, not too successfully, with a jest on passing the
International Date Line: "Gone, November 5th, 1878, a *dies
non*, which never was born. Lost, strayed, or stolen—a rare
diadem, composed of twenty-four precious gems—some diamond bright, some rubies rare, some jet as black as night. It
was to have been displayed at midnight, but when looked for
it was nowhere to be found."[12] He comes out somewhat better
soon afterwards following a passage in which he grows enthusiastic about the beauties of a night at sea. It ends, "One does
feel in such moments, when beauty and sublimity are over-
poweringly displayed, that there are worlds and life beyond
our ken." The next day's entry opens with: "I know I went to
bed sometime early this morning, but after reading last night's
effusion in the cold, sober light of day, it strikes me I must
have been rather enthusiastic."[13]

In his predictions, which are few, Carnegie comes out right
about half the time in *Round the World*. For instance, he
appears to have been correct that "America will continue to
lead in fast horses,"[14] and in asserting that "by and by" Japan
would adopt a representative government (49). He didn't do
so well in predicting that America would not soon be exporting
live cattle (5); that it would within a short time and for the
foreseeable future have no federal taxes but on luxuries (9);
or that there would not be more than a few hundred miles of
railway in Japan "for centuries" (70).

In general, Carnegie's travel writing, except for promoting
his ideas, is straightforward and factual. But there are moments

of emotion, humor, or—as Winkler describes them—"pure ec-
stasy."[15] In his description of the burning ghat, for instance,
Carnegie writes: "My heart bled for a poor widow whose husband had just been taken to the pile. She was of very low
caste, but her grief was heartrending; not loud, but I thought
I could taste the saltness of her tears, they seemed so bitter"
(210). On the other hand, he can cap a thrilling tale with a
bit of his inward prejudice that makes it almost ridiculous:
perhaps—like the knocking on the gates in *Macbeth*—to relieve
tension. After telling the story of Jessie, the heroine of Lucknow,
he adds: "I have been hesitating whether the next paragraph
in my notebook should go down here or be omitted. Probably
it would be in better taste if quietly ignored, but then it would
be so finely natural to put in. Well, I shall be natural or nothing,
and recount that I could not help rejoicing that Jessie was
Scotch, and that Scotchmen first broke the rebels' lines and
reached the fort, and that the bagpipes led the way. That's all.
I feel better now that this is also set down" (229). With that
he passes on to a discussion of Lucknow's lack of fine buildings.

Perhaps the most highly praised passage in all his writings
was created after he had reluctantly gone to see the Taj Mahal
by moonlight, fearing he would be disappointed. He opens the
next diary entry:

We have seen it, but I am without the slightest desire to burst
into rapturous adjectives. Do not expect me to attempt a description
of it, or to try to express my feelings. There are some subjects too
sacred for analysis, or even for words, and I now know that there
is a human structure so exquisitely fine, or unearthly, as to lift it into
this holy domain. Let me say little about it; only tell you that,
lingering until the sun went down, we turned in the noble gateway
which forms a frame through which you see the Taj in the distance,
with only the blue sky in the background, around and above it, and
there took our last fond sad farewell, as the shades of night were
wrapping the lovely jewel in their embrace, as if it were a charge too
sweetly precious not to be safely enveloped in night's black mantle,
till it could again shine forth at the dawn in all its beauty to adorn
the earth. . . . But till the day I die, amid mountain streams or moonlight strolls in the forest wherever and whenever the mood comes,
when all that is most sacred, most elevated, and most pure recur

to shed their radiance upon the tranquil mind; there will be found among my treasures the memory of that lovely charm—the Taj. (252–53)

One very important thing the trip around the world did for Carnegie, which was to have a lasting effect on his life: it gave him an entirely new attitude toward religion. "A new horizon was opened up to me by this voyage," he wrote later in his *Autobiography*. "It quite changed my intellectual outlook. . . . The result of my journey was to bring a certain mental peace. Where there had been chaos there was now order. . . . All the remnants of theology in which I had been born and bred . . . now ceased to influence my thoughts. I found that no nation had all the truth in the revelation it regards as divine, and no tribe is so low as to be left without some truth."[16]

II Our Coaching Trip

Carnegie's second book of travel, *Our Coaching Trip*, was, like *Round the World*, written for the amusement of his close friends, and discloses the fact even more thoroughly than the earlier work, by playfulness and numerous personal references. Its dedication "to my brother and trusty associates" is almost the same as that of its predecessor. It is a happy, simple, and straightforward account of a trip from "Brighton to Inverness,"[17] driving four-in-hand in a coach with ten companions, including his mother. The trip, measuring eight hundred thirty-one miles, took forty-eight days elapsed time. But this figure includes sixteen on which no traveling was done, leaving thirty-two days for coaching—an average of just under twenty-six miles a day, with time for regular luncheon stops and much sight-seeing.[18] Included in the party were "Lady Dowager, Mother, Head of the Clan (no Salic Law in our family); Miss Jeannie Johns (Prima Donna); Miss Alice French (Stewardess); Mr. and Mrs. Mc-Cargo (Dainty Davie); Mr. and Mrs. King (Paisley Troubadours, Aleck good for fun and Angie good for everything); Benjamin F. Vandevort (Benjie); Henry Phipps, Jr. (H. P., our Pard); G. F. McCandless (General Manager); ten in all, making together with the scribe the All-coaching Eleven."[19]

McCargo was one of the "Scotties" of his Pittsburgh boyhood, and later his superintendent of telegraphy in railroad days. King and Phipps were associates in steelmaking, as was Gardiner McCandless. The two girls were friends (Miss Johns a singer and Miss French in charge of luncheons) and Vandevort was the younger brother of John, who had gone with Carnegie on the tour of Europe and the trip around the world. Carnegie had also invited Louise Whitfield, later to become his bride. She wished to accept, but was prevented by the frown of Margaret Carnegie, who recognized her as the first real threat to the mother's complete domination of her son.[20]

Our Coaching Trip is almost exactly the same length as Carnegie's earlier book, not counting a fifty-three-page quotation from the Dunfermline papers concerning his stop there near the end of July for his mother to lay the cornerstone of a free library he was giving to the city.[21] It displays almost all the typical Carnegie themes, including—besides those of *Round the World*—admiration for Great Britain, maternal devotion, ascendency of Anglo-Saxon blood, interest in economics, unflinching faith in democracy, hatred of imperialism and speculation, and love of peace.

The book opens in almost exactly the same way as its predecessor: "Bang! click! once more the desk closes and the key turns! Not 'Round the World' again, but 'Ho for England, for England!' is the cry, and 'Scotland's hills and Scotland's dales and Scotland's vales for me.'" (2). Again, as if feeling the need for a precedent, Carnegie cites the time in 1865 when he, his cousin "Dod" (George Lauder, Jr.), Henry Phipps, and John Vandevort had "walked through Southern England with knapsacks on our backs" (1). Andrew had then announced that some day "when my 'ships come home,' I should drive a party of my dearest friends from Brighton to Inverness." Somewhat defensively he points out that he made this statement before the appearance of *Adventures of a Phaeton*, by William Black, whom he would take on a later coaching trip.

Immediately, however, Carnegie turns to a long philosophical digression on the realization of "air-castles"—a charming though somewhat overextended passage of almost 2,000 words which passes from whimsey into allegory. It begins with—and was un-

doubtedly inspired by—the absence of John Vandevort, who
on the walking trip had exclaimed how if he ever achieved
an income of $1,500 a year he would give up work forever:
" 'Catch me working any more like a slave, as you and Harry
do!' Well, well, Vandy's air-castle was fifteen hundred dollars
a year, yet see him now when thousands roll in upon him
every month. Hard at it still—and see the goddess Fortune laugh-
ing in her sleeve at the good joke on Vandy. He has his air-
castle, but doesn't recognize the structure" (2–3).

It is uncertain, and speculation on the point would be futile,
whether Carnegie had definite friends in mind as he goes on
to speak of *Miss Fashion*, the speculator, and the society
woman, although the definite details in the first case might indicate she was a real person, the others less probably so (3–8).
At the end of the passage, as with his description of a night at
sea in *Round the World*,[22] he brings the reader back to the
story by tweaking his own nose: "I am as bad as Sterne in his
'Sentimental Journey,' and will never get on at this rate" (8).

The start from Brighton was made on June 17 after a brief
visit to London. Instead of eleven passengers as planned, the
group totaled fifteen, in addition to Perry, the coachman, and
Joe, the footman. The Kings were to meet the coach later,
after taking their children to visit grandparents at Paisley,
and their places were temporarily taken by Carnegie's cousin,
Maggie Lauder, and Emma Franks of Liverpool, sister of his
companion on the 1865 trip through Europe. After coaxing the
host a bit, the latter was added as a permanent member of the
party. In addition, a Londoner, Theodore Beck and his daughter,
and Mr. and Mrs. Thomas Graham from Wolverhampton began
the journey with the "Charioteers." Beck left the coach at
Windsor, the second day, but was replaced by his son for
five days. The Becks stopped at Banbury, and the Grahams at
Wolverhampton, where the visitors were entertained in homes
instead of at an inn. The Kings had rejoined the party at Banbury, and at Wolverhampton the McCargos, Miss Johns and
young Vandevort left for two weeks for a trip to Paris, to return
at Carlisle. There were other occasional brief changes in the
party (25, 27, 107–108, 149–50).

Carnegie expanded the first day's journey to about 7,500

words with a rather complete account of the arrangements, interlarded so neatly with literary quotations and jokes and incidents that it is as readable as the rest. Instead of—or in addition to—advance reading for the trip, he had armed himself with guidebooks on some of the towns (54, 90).

The narrative runs well, with description, incident, serious discussion, and humor (which is very rare in Carnegie's other writing) well proportioned and distributed. There are some choice tidbits, such as one Carnegie inserts in his discussion of Coventry, home of Godiva and George Eliot:

A friend told me that a lady friend of hers, who was staying at the hotel in Florence where George Eliot was, made her acquaintance casually without knowing her name. Something, she knew not what, attracted her to her, and after a few days she began sending flowers to the strange woman. Completely fascinated, she went almost daily for hours to sit with her. This continued for many days, the lady using the utmost freedom, and not without feeling that the attention was pleasing to the queer, plain, and unpretending Englishwoman. One day she discovered by chance who her companion really was. Never before, as she said, had she felt such mortification. She went timidly to George Eliot's room and took her hand in hers, but shrank back unable to speak, while the tears rolled down her cheeks. "What is wrong?" was asked, and then the explanation came, "I didn't know who you were. I never suspected *it was you.*" Then came George Eliot's turn to be embarrassed. "You did not know that I was George Eliot, but you were drawn to plain me all for my own self, a woman? I am so happy." She kissed the American lady tenderly, and the true friendship thus formed knew no end, but ripened to the close. (89)

A few pages later appears one of the characteristic expressions of the philosophy which was more and more beginning to shape Carnegie into the man the world remembers:

In this world we must learn not to lay up our treasures, but to enjoy them day by day as we travel the path we never return to. If we fail in this we shall find when we do come to the days of leisure that we have lost the taste for and the capacity to enjoy them. There are so many unfortunates cursed with plenty to retire upon, but with nothing to retire to! Sound wisdom that the schoolboy displayed who did not "believe in putting away for tomorrow the cake he could eat today." It might not be fresh on the morrow, or the cat might steal it. The cat steals many a choice bit from Americans intended for the morrow. Among the saddest of all spectacles to me is that of an elderly man occupying his last years grasping for more dollars. (95)

The party entered Scotland July 16, and from this point onward there are frequent references to the various Scottish heroes and their doings, to replace the previous comment on the currently great men of England. At one halt, the seventy-two-year-old Margaret Morrison Carnegie and Mrs. King had waded barefoot in the brook, and "kilted their petticoats and danced a highland reel on the greensward, in sight of the company, but at some distance from us" (122). Surprisingly little is said of Mrs. Carnegie after they crossed the border. Perhaps she was overcome by emotion. But there Carnegie records his unforgettable sentiment: "It's a God's mercy I was born a Scotchman, for I do not see how I could ever have been contented to be anything else" (152). For the moment his adulation of America was silenced. But not for long.

No other work of Carnegie—not even the *Autobiography*—gives such a complete look at the man himself as *Our Coaching Trip*, nor such a glimpse at his broad literary reading. During its first fifty pages he refers to or inserts quotations from Henry Scott Riddell, Shakespeare, Burns, Wordsworth, Coleridge, William Black, Elizabeth Barrett Browning, Thomas Carlyle, William Cullen Bryant, the Bible, John G. Saxe, Lawrence Sterne, Pope, Homer, Aesop, Thomas Campbell, William Dean Howells, Thomas H. Huxley, Oliver Goldsmith, Tennyson, Izaak Walton, "Josh Billings" (Henry W. Shaw), Walter Scott, Matthew and Edwin Arnold, William Winter, Artemus Ward, John S. Kennedy, W. Robertson Smith, Robert Ingersoll, William Clark, Milton, *Harper's Magazine, Fortnightly Review, Nineteenth Century,* and the *Encyclopaedia Britannica.* The fact that a good many of the quotations show slight variation from the original might indicate that they were written from memory, without checking.

Unlike *Round the World, Our Coaching Trip* was not written during the trip, although in accordance with the day's style in travel books it is set down and arranged in diary style. Carnegie described its production:

All the notes I made of the coaching trip were a few lines a day in twopenny pass-books bought before we started. As with "Round the World", I thought that I might some day write a magazine article, or give some account of my excursion for those who accompanied me: but one wintry day I decided that it was scarcely worth while to go down to the New York office, three miles distant, and the question was how I should occupy the spare time. I thought of the coaching trip, and decided to write a few lines just to see how I should get on. The narrative flowed freely, and before the day was over I had written between three and four thousand words. I took up the pleasing task every stormy day when it was unnecessary for me to visit the office, and in exactly twenty sittings I had finished a book.[23]

III   An American Four-in-Hand in Britain

In some respects, Carnegie's adaptations of *Round the World* and *Our Coaching Trip* from private publications for friends to trade books are as revealing and of as great interest as the original works themselves. He tells how it all began: "I handed the notes [manuscript of *Our Coaching Trip*] to Scribners' people and asked them to print a few hundred copies for private circulation. The volume pleased my friends, as 'Round the World' had done. Mr. [John D.] Champlin one day told me that Mr. [Charles] Scribner had read the book and would very much like to publish it for general circulation upon his own account, subject to a royalty. The vain author is easily persuaded that what he has done is meritorious, and I consented."[24] Apparently he noted later, as it is bracketed in the published *Autobiography*: "Every year this still nets me a small sum in royalties. And thirty years have gone by, 1912."[25]

But the change from a private to a public book was not so light a matter as Carnegie would make it sound, or perhaps as he recalled it many years afterward. A comparison of *Our Coaching Trip* with the trade version, retitled *An American*

Four-in-Hand in Britain, shows extensive changes. Somewhat oversimplifying, he explains in the preface: "The original intent of the book must be the excuse for the highly personal nature of the narrative, which could scarcely be changed without an entire remodelling, a task for which the writer had neither time nor inclination; so with the exception of a few suppressions and some additions which seemed necessary under its new conditions, its character has not been materially altered."[26]

Careful collation of *Our Coaching Trip* with *An American Four-in-Hand* reveals scores of changes, but a majority of these are relatively minor; initials instead of names; variation in punctuation; change of tense; switch in word order, or other such details. Ignoring these, there remain sixty-seven principal differences, including fifty-eight insertions of more than a few words, three changes (two to correct minor errors, the other on the ground of taste), and six omissions. All the omissions are of personal material, varying from a few lines to the fifty-three-page quotation of stories on the stop at Dunfermline, referred to above.

Insertions are principally of two kinds: twenty-two are of what might be referred to as "guidebook material"—not taken directly from such sources, but descriptive and historical matter of the kind usually found in guidebooks; sixteen are inserted to give the author a chance to present his ideas on religion, economics, political science, and similar matters; eleven are casual material (mostly from a few lines to a paragraph) on weather, travel conditions and contrasts between Britain and America; four are transitional, to smooth over omitted or changed passages; three are humorous incidents and two poetical quotations.

Many of the "guidebook" and "idea" inserts are of considerable length, so that the text (originally about 66,000 words without the Dunfermline quotations) is increased by about a third, to some 87,000 words. In general the changes are wisely made, and tend to improve the style and interest of the book, and its appeal to the public. The first edition, 2,000 copies, was immediately sold, and within the next few years it was reprinted eighteen times, sales reaching almost 15,000—a considerable figure for that day.[27]

IV   Round the World *(Trade Book)*

In revising *Our Coaching Trip* for the public, Carnegie—never one to underestimate his own prospects—may have expected a public edition of *Round the World* to follow, since his first omission was the slap-dash opening which was almost identical with that of his earlier work.[28] He retained the opening in his revision of the Scribner's edition of *Round the World,* which proved considerably more extensive than that of its mate.

Disregarding minor variations, this revision totaled 123 instances, including eighty-eight additions, twenty-six changes, and nine omissions. Six of the latter were deletions of personal material, two were to avoid repetition, and one to facilitate a transition.

Twelve of the changes were to correct errors, ten were to improve style, one to soften a comment on religion and one to update the previous text. The other two are puzzling, and similar: the first, in his apostrophe to Burns, substitutes *A Man's a Man for a' That* and *My Nannie's Awa'* for *Tam O'Shanter* and *To a Daisy;*[29] the other, in commenting on differing tastes in music, puts *Lohengrin* in place of *My Nannie's Awa'.*[30] The additions include thirty-one of "guidebook material," twenty-two on politics and economics, fifteen on religion, nine for miscellaneous comments, four each for humor and to update earlier references, and three for clarity. Even the choice of guidebook material is significant, including principally data suited to illustrate or prepare the way for his principles and ideas. With this revision, Carnegie's writing had come of age, using books to promote his ideas, as he had formerly used letters to newspapers.

Carnegie evidently planned the expanded version with care, increasing the space for each part of the trip almost always in proportion to the number of pages in the first edition. Thus, the transcontinental journey goes from eleven pages to thirteen, the voyage from seventeen to twenty-two, Japan from nineteen to twenty-five, the coasting trip from eleven to fifteen, China from forty-nine to seventy-one, Malaysia from eleven to seventeen, the Ceylon trip from eight to twenty, India from sixty-three to 100, the Suez journey from six to nineteen, Egypt from ten to twenty, Italy from six to fourteen, and the conclusion is enlarged only two pages, from fifteen to seventeen. Since it would have been simple and easy to expand the volume by restoring the Scandinavian trip and other parts omitted from the early printing, it is evident that Carnegie's intent was to promote his ideas and beliefs, not merely to increase the number of pages.

The expanded *Round the World* was published in 1884 in New York and London.[31] As a trade book, it did not prove so successful as *An American Four-in-Hand*. It was reprinted eight times, at least until 1902, sales totaling about 5,000 copies.[32]

While it cannot be said that Carnegie added a new dimension to travel writing—such books had been used for many years to promote ideas and policies—he did push this phase farther than most of his contemporaries, and more successfully in the sense of using ideas without detracting from the readability of the work.

CHAPTER 4

Millionaire Journalist: 1882-1916

ANDREW Carnegie's career as a journalist, like some of his other successful ventures, apparently had its origin in a chance event. Yet it is also probable that he would have eventually come to magazine articles as an outgrowth of his lifelong habit of writing letters to newspapers. Certainly one who could say "Dynamite is a child's toy compared to the press," and "The weapon of Republicanism is not the sword, but the pen,"[1] could hardly have ignored the rising magazine field for long.

His delay until he was past forty-five was partly due to the fact that the modern type of magazine, for which Carnegie eventually wrote so many of his articles, is a recent development, dating back little more than a century. Those few which were founded before the close of the Civil War were usually short lived and of minor influence. Before 1870 most of the ones which did prove successful were devoted principally to belles lettres, a field for which he was poorly prepared, and sometimes biography and travel, in which his interests were limited.

From childhood days Carnegie had been an avid reader of newspapers, and after reaching manhood a constant writer of letters to their editors. In 1868 his dream of retirement from business had included, "purchase a controlling interest in some newspaper or live review and give the general management of it attention, taking a part in public matters...."[2]

At the height of his interest in British politics, from 1881 to 1885, Carnegie joined Samuel Storey and Passmore Edwards in setting up a syndicate of radical papers to support William E. Gladstone and fight to abolish the monarchy and House of Lords. But he did little if any writing for the seven daily and ten weekly journals in which he and his partners held controlling interest. At last, in the backlash which followed the passage of the Reform Bill of 1884, he saw the futility of his effort and disposed of all but a few of his holdings in the field, dropping any serious involvement, though not all his equity was liquidated until 1902. In later years he referred to the venture as part of sowing his wild oats.[3]

It was soon after the beginning of this period of newspaper publishing that Carnegie entered what was to prove his most fruitful field of literature—contributing to the magazines.

I First Essay at Journalism

As with so many of his activities, the opportunity came by chance—almost by accident. In his years of becoming a lion in London, Carnegie had formed a lifelong friendship with John Morley, editor of *Fortnightly Review*, for many years one of Britain's most prestigious liberal journals. The coaching trip from Brighton to Inverness was creating attention, and someone suggested it might serve for an article. It was natural that Carnegie would offer the finished piece to his friend, even if Morley was not in the company when the suggestion was made. Carnegie, as usual seeking to justify his entering a new field, began the article by reporting the matter: " 'Why don't you give us, in one of our reviews, some account of your coaching trip . . . and tell us what your dozen of American guests thought of us? I'm sure it would be interesting.' Upon this hint I write." The question may possibly have been asked and the article arranged with the idea that the account would be a recital of his guests' reactions to the scenery, hospitality, and occasional incidents of the journey. Carnegie was beginning his drive to reform Britain and overthrow the monarchy. And as was his custom, he took the suggestion in the way he wanted it, if not in the sense in which it had been made. But he was careful to hedge by pointing out a ground for his interpretation: "The speaker was a noted politician—one busy with affairs of state—and, therefore, in this article I shall confine myself to the impression which political questions made upon the minds of my Republican friends."[4]

He opens softly, with a charming and complimentary paragraph on the trip—perhaps designed as a peace offering, but more likely (for Carnegie seldom wrote without weighing his words and their effect)—to provide maximum shock when his criticisms began: "Indeed, it would be impossible in one article to do more than consider one of the many interesting subjects the journey suggests; nor could any article tell how delightful, beyond all anticipation, our excursion through your quietly beautiful island proved to be, while the happiness, the joyousness of the party from beginning to end is not to be described by words. Suffice it to say that the experiment has left us all unable to think of any mode of spending our coming summers which is not tame and insipid in comparison with coaching through Britain."[5]

Stage set, Carnegie immediately plunges into his criticism of the political situation in Britain:

1. Whereas in the new land, fundamental principles of government were all settled, in "this so-called old and settled land there was nothing settled whatever, and the people were in a ferment, satisfied with nothing." (156–58)

2. Americans were surprised by discussion of the Land question, and to learn of entail and primogeniture, and that a man renting land is not allowed to clear it of game, if he desires.

3. Members of the party were shocked at seeing an established church clergyman in prison at Lancaster "because he conscientiously thought it wrong, in his ministry, to wear something or not to wear it. . . ." (158–59)

4. They were surprised to learn that even the House of Commons was the subject of severe criticism because of unfair and unequal election laws. (159–60)

5. They were surprised at problems with the courts, and that English legal institutions represented, not "the people" but "His Majesty." (160–61)

6. The party was much disturbed over the Irish question, felt that it should be settled in the way that of Scotland had been, by allowing home rule within the United Kingdom. (161–62)

7. Then he took up the question of tariff and free trade, arguing it at some length. (162–64)

8. And at last, the question of the monarchy and hereditary privilege. (164–65)

Sketching out the uncertainty of political matters in England, Carnegie describes how, during the Land Bill excitement which was going on at the time of the trip, many people were calling for the abolition of the House of Lords. He continues:

This seemed to [my friend] revolutionary. Imagine a proposition in America to abolish the Senate. While total abolition would be deprecated by the company, still the more moderate opinion would seem to be that a radical change in the constitution of the House of Lords was bound to take place ere long. And the subject would be dismissed with the remark that "if the Lords set themselves up against the opinion of the country," or, as it was gently put by one speaker, did not "behave themselves (*i.e.* register the decrees of the Commons), they would be swept away." . . . Of course, the American . . . had heard that an Englishman "dearly loved a lord," and now he doubts it. "Why don't they elect their Second Chamber somewhat as we do, and then it would have some real power, as springing from the people like the Commons?" . . . That was what one of my friends wanted to know, but I could not very well answer his question. (157–58)

Carnegie seldom resorted to irony or ridicule. But he is hitting pretty hard, and in regard to the jailed clergyman, he writes—

I did what I could to explain to my indignant friends how heinous Mr. Greene's offense had been, inasmuch as he had made a "bargain" with the State to worship God as the State directed, but the word "bargain" only created more disgust, and my friends left the prison saying, "And this is England! Shame!" This incident was not easily effaced from the minds of the Americans, and Church and State presented a frequent topic of conversation. (159)

Only on the final point did Carnegie release the pressure:

I have purposely left the only remaining political edifice till the last. The *Throne itself.* Surely here is something so high as to float in serene calm above the storms. . . . Such, however, was not the impression received by my American friends. (164)

He goes on to point out that while there was considerable

agitation against the whole system of hereditary privilege, and even the monarchy, the great majority of the people who had expressed an opinion were loyal to Queen Victoria herself. "This thought pleased my American friends, and allowed them to claim that she was "just the same as if she had been elected," and therefore "a good-enough Republican" (164).

Then came the whirlwind finish:

In conclusion, if the constitution of the Second Chamber is in danger, if even the House of Commons is on the eve of decided changes, if the tenure of the very soil of the realm is unsatisfactory, if the system of law is to be recast, if the sacred Church itself is a bone of contention . . . and if the throne itself be dependent upon the personal character of one man; in short, if England is not pleased with any of her political institutions, was it any wonder that the sympathies of my American friends were deeply touched by the sad spectacle of a dissatisfied, divided, wrangling people, irritated by the pressure of old forms. . . . (165)

The solution for Carnegie, of course, is to change Britain to a republican system of government. With this hope for Britain, "a happy issue out of all her troubles," the Americans had sailed for America with "feelings warmed and quickened into fond affection for the old home." While Carnegie had not yet solved the problem of how to win friends and influence people in such situations, he was evidently seeking.

II *Early Rebuff*

Having tasted success, Carnegie lost no time in trying again. Back in Britain to manage his newspaper syndicate and push his liberal ideas, he fired off another article to the *Fortnightly*.[6] But Morley had resigned to go into politics almost immediately after the publication of "As Others See Us," being succeeded by T. H. S. Escott. The article was apparently rejected, since it was never published. Perhaps Carnegie's hurt was so great that he never tried the magazine again. At least nothing else by him ever appeared in its pages.

Two more years passed before he succeeded in getting into print again in a leading journal. This time it was *Macmillan's*

Magazine. The story, "The Oil and Gas Wells of Pennsylvania," was completely noncontroversial—largely an account of his participation in the early oil strikes at the Storey Farm, and of the discovery of gas around Pittsburgh some fifteen years later. He described the great Haymaker gas well at Murrysville, and other strikes forming almost a circle around the city.

Despite the work of completing *Triumphant Democracy,* (1886) Carnegie succeeded in turning out a story on a related theme for the first issue of the *North American Review* in 1886, and two more on the labor question for the newly founded *Forum* in April and August, before suffering his worst illness and the loss of his mother and brother that autumn. Recovery and his subsequent marriage so took up his time that only an interview in the *New York Times* and a published speech appear to have come to wide public notice. But in 1889 Carnegie attained his full stride again, with three articles in *North American Review,* a report on the Pan American Conference, to which he was a delegate, and a published address on *Pennsylvania's Industries and Railroad Policy,* given March 18 before the Franklin Institute.[7]

III   *Sudden Popularity*

The second of these articles Carnegie titled simply "Wealth," and with it his journalistic labors hit their high-water mark. Reprinted in England, it was given the caption, "The Gospel of Wealth," and quickly became famous, catapulting its author into worldwide prominence. Reprinted with other essays and one speech as a book under the new title in 1900, it became his best known and most successful work.[8]

No longer did Carnegie have to seek outlets for his opinions. They were besought on every hand, and from that time forth he contributed a stream of articles to leading (and occasionally to little known) periodicals in America and Britain. Some were reprinted in later books or editions or in pamphlet form. His output was not large—never more than five in one year—but it was steady. During the twenty-three years from 1889 to 1911 inclusive, he published fifty-seven magazine articles, not counting interviews, letters to editors, or published speeches. In 1887 Carnegie's income had been $1,800,000,[9] so obviously any remuneration received from his writing was relatively unimportant. Yet there is nothing to indicate that he was reluctant to accept the money, which to him was a part of the assurance that his writing was considered of value, not merely used in order to capitalize on his name. In his *Autobiography*[10] he wrote with evident satisfaction of the royalties received from books. And long after retiring as one of the world's richest men to give away his fortune, he indicated he was still being paid for his literary work. Writing to his cousin, Dod, who had taken up painting, he commented: "Yes, you are at last an artist. As an artist I too am in demand. My painting is word painting and I'm all 'ordered' and 'sold'. Folk maun do something for their bread."[11]

Carnegie's total magazine record, counted as above, shows sixty-eight articles, forty-six in American and twenty-two in British publications.[12] Twenty-nine of these dealt in one way or another with political matters, thirty-three with economics. Prior to 1890 his interests appear to be chiefly in finance, with only two out of eight articles concerned with politics. During the troubled years from 1890 through 1905 there was a sudden upsurge of writing on British, American, and international political affairs, totaling twenty, with only fifteen on economics. During the final eleven years of his writing Carnegie had only eight on politics, and eleven on economics.

Of his total, twenty-five—a little more than one-third—were later printed in book form in his lifetime, thirteen in *The Gospel of Wealth,* eleven in *The Empire of Business,* and one in *Problems of Today.* All but six of these articles were on economics. A number of others on both disciplines were circulated in pamphlet form.

IV   *Four Related Articles*

Four articles on closely related matters provide an interesting insight into the manner in which Carnegie clung to his convictions and pursued his ends over a period of more than two decades. These are: "Do Americans Hate England?" (*North American Review,* June, 1890); "Does America Hate England?" (*Contemporary Review,* November, 1897); "Britain and Her

Offspring" (*Nineteenth Century*, May, 1911) and "Arbitration" (*Contemporary Review*, August, 1911.)

The first of these formed the second part of a symposium by seven principal Americans[13] in reply to "The Hatred of England," a rather intemperate blast in the May, 1890, issue of *North American Review*, by Goldwin Smith. Carnegie went into the question rather more at length than most of the others, beginning logically with a distinction between the attitudes of adult Americans and schoolboys fired up by history lessons about the Revolution, and between hatred and dislike. He then took up the question of rivalry, pointing out that the masses of British people liked America, but that the privileged classes resented its danger to their position. He dismissed as mere equality what Smith had declared an affront—that James G. Blaine dropped the traditional "America ventures to hope . . ." in favor of the Briton's curt, "Her Majesty expects that. . . ." In conclusion he cited one of his traditional themes, asserting that despite rivalries and other differences, England and America are father and son, both feeling keenly that "blood is thicker than water."

Seven years later the same question was being discussed, and through a British journal Carnegie approached it in much the same fashion as before; first the matter of competition, then switching immediately to the matter of *race*. Pointing out that the United States had recently challenged Britain's refusal to arbitrate a territorial dispute with Venezuela, he quoted the statement of a member of the Senate: "This is our own race . . .; of course, we have difficulty of our own with her, and we do not intend to let even our Motherland light the torch of war upon our continent . . . but this is a little family matter between ourselves. It does not mean that German, Russian, Frenchmen or any foreigners may combine to attack our race to its destruction, without counting us in. No, sir-ee."

He then took up the two principal bones of contention—the Venezuelan question and the killing of seals—on their merits, asserting that America was in the right in both instances, concluding with an assurance of friendliness, based on common race.

The third article, in another American periodical, without directly raising the former question, pointed out how Canada, Australia, and other British dominions were patterning their institutions more upon the United States than the British system, predicting that "From this time forth the dear old Mother and her children are to draw closer together ... until our entire English-speaking race enjoy the blessings flowing from government founded upon the equality of the citizen, one man's privilege every man's right." At the end of the essay, adding a section which he dated as the time of reading the proof, he burst into a paean of happiness at the announcement that the two nations had agreed to proclaim that all international disputes should be submitted to arbitration. He concluded with the mother-wife theme that would be so common in his biographies:[14] "Should the writer be spared to see his native land and adopted lands—Motherland and Wifeland—united hand in hand ... life will possess for him a charm unknown before ... almost leading him to murmur with bowed head, 'Now let thy servant depart in peace.' "[15]

Carnegie opened the fourth article—evidently inspired by the same event as the peroration of the third, directly with his pet theme of the importance of race: "History confirms the claim that the abolition of war between civilized nations by arbitration of all disputes is emphatically the mission of the English-speaking race." Briefly citing previous difficulties between Britain and America, Carnegie urged the frequent practice of what now bears the name of *summitry,* noting, "That we only hate those we do not know is good as a general rule." Then, referring to the exception in most previous arbitration treaties for "questions affecting 'honour' or vital 'interest,' " he argued: "The first subject reserved *i.e.,* that of Honour, is the most dishonoured word in the language. No country ever did, or ever could dishonour another. No man ever did, or ever could, dishonour another. It is impossible. All Honour's wounds are self-inflicted."

Urging the enormous cost of war—"Ruinous though this may be, it is as dust in the balance compared with its sin"—he went into a discussion of the decline of slavery and the duel. He cited the experience of his own Hero Fund to prove that doing away with war would not end heroism. Then, characteristically, he related an argument with Gladstone over the first

Irish Home rule Bill, quoted and paraphrased Burns, and
concluded: "Just as it was with slavery and with duelling,
when our race banishes war within its wide boundaries, as
it is on the eve of doing, it sounds its death knell. Long may my
native and adopted lands (Motherland and Wifeland) hand
in hand, lead the world to its upward and onward march to
higher and higher stages of civilisation [sic], tending to make
earth a heaven, which is the mission of our race. Let us falter
not!"

Had he been a younger man, and had the onset of World
War I been delayed a few years, there is little doubt that
Carnegie would have expanded this series into a book on the
attainment of peace. It could have included his brief article in
Outlook[16] proposing a league of nations; *A League of Peace*,
his Rectorial Address at St. Andrews University;[17] "The Cry of
'Wolf' ";[18] "Peace Versus War: The President's Solution";[19] and
"The Decadence of Militarism."[20]

V *Creative Efforts*

Carnegie seldom attempted anything but straight, formal
prose. The few instances in which he tried verse were all
brief and on the ludicrous side, except for a revision of the old
Ballad of Sir Patrick Spens, for his little daughter, to give it a
happy ending.[21] The result indicates that if he had tried poesy
seriously, he might have done reasonably well. He is also said to
have amused his daughter for hours at a time with antic tales,
most of which he invented.[22]

One most interesting departure from his usual style is "Britain's
Appeal to the Gods,"[23] a friendly but not-too-gentle satire on
England's imperialism and high tariff, while seeking to get
lower rates from America and other nations. At the head of
the article the magazine editor published an extract of the
author's letter explaining his purpose in writing on the subject,
but saying nothing as to why he used his novel approach and
style: "My aim has been to show your countrymen how absurdly
grasping they are, how *unreasonable*. Never has the world seen
such a nation, and there is much excuse for the feeling that
Britain is entitled to continue to inherit the earth. She still

wants more, when what surprises everyone conversant with her position is how she ever succeeded in getting and doing so much. I am impressed every time I look into the figures."[24]

The whole article is cast as an appeal by Britain, taking up, point by point and addressed to the various appropriate Olympians, the instances and statistics of the nation's greedy actions and attitudes. For each she is rebuked and answered by *Chorus*—obviously the author—until near the end, when Britain cries out, evidently in despair, to know the future. This time the answer is reassuring. But when more definite information is sought, no answer is given, and Carnegie—*in propria persona*—closes with a message of hope and confidence.

The article opens:

Hear us! hear us! mighty Jove, and ye dread gods who dwell upon Olympus.

Mark ye, our Foreign Commerce is only 903,363,000£. per year.

Chorus.—Ungrateful favourite of the gods! It never was so great either in Imports or Exports. No nation ever approached it in amount. *Per capita* it is 21£. 10*s*. France has only 8£. 11*s*. 9*d*.; Germany 8£. 6*s*. 8*d*.; United States, 6£. 3*s*.

Neptune, great god of the Sea, and thou, Triton the Trumpeter!

Mark ye, Guardians of Britannia's rule over the waves, our Shipping is only 16,600,000 tons.

Chorus.—Insatiate greed! It never was so great and is constantly increasing. All the other nations combined have not as much. Beware lest thine ingratitude offend the gods. . . . Thou wert first; now others build ships and must share with thee.

There follow appeals to "Midas, great king of Gold," for greater national wealth; Vulcan for an increase in iron, steel and coal production; Deucalion, god of Increase, for greater population; Minerva, goddess of the loom, for a greater share of the spinning industry; "Jupiter, and all the gods together," asking why rivals increase faster (the answer ending with, "Cease to be children crying for the moon"); Ceres for greater food production; and again to Jupiter, seeking to know destiny, and asking to be preserved from becoming "a fifth-rate power." The answer: "No such destiny for thy race impends. . . . Be of

good cheer and of stout heart. Let this suffice; trust the gods.
Farewell!"

The piece ends in a double conclusion:

Stay! Stay! Let us know more! How? When? What shall we do?
Muta, goddess of silence, floated above. No audible response
came, but the babbling air seemed to spread abroad in whispering
sounds—"Seek to know no more: how all is to be wrought lieth upon
the lap of the gods; to the one mortal who has presumed to forecast
their plans we waft this message: 'Thy lips are sealed.'"
So keeps the mortal his own sweet reveries, happy in the knowledge
that for his native land all is well, since all is to be better than yet has
been, which is saying much, and for his race—the English-speaking
race (language makes race)—its future is far to surpass its past.
To it the gods have decreed the leadership of the world for the
good of the world. The day of its power is not afar. There be many
who read these lines who shall behold its dawn.[25]

Considering the friendly acceptance by the editor, and
Carnegie's success in the novel presentation of his theme, it
is surprising that he seems never to have tried another such
radical departure from his usual journalistic style.

VI *Final Contributions*

Rarely even in his final decade did Carnegie bother to write
on anything but serious subjects. His principal concerns during
this period were peace, labor, the tariff, international affairs,
and hereditary transmission of property. But on one occasion he
unbent enough to write "Doctor Golf" for the *Independent*.[26]
Like several of his other essays during those years, he used
his beloved simplified spelling, as in: "We are under the sky,
worshipers of the 'God of the Open Air.' Every breth seems to
drive away weakness and diseas, securing for us longer terms
of happy days here on earth, even bringing something of heven
here to us." It is a charming bit, opening with some history on
the introduction of golf into America (from Scotland, and by
Dunfermline Scots, of course). Then he recites how it was
originally a game for the wealthy, and talks of its pleasures,
introducing some amusing incidents, emphasizing that golf en-

courages friendly rivalries and requires concentration and is good exercise.

Carnegie's last publication, three years before his death, returns to the one great purpose of his life, and is titled "Principles of Giving."[27] It differs little from what he had written and said on the same subject in his early retirement years.

VII *Summary*

Looking over Carnegie's production as a journalist, we become aware that it shows only minor changes in the more than three decades of his activity in this field, or even in a much longer period of his life. Even his language and style vary little from things he wrote in his youth. In "Wealth" in 1889 he once uses "bequested" for "bequeathed" as he had in his letter about library use in 1853. In his "Gospel of Wealth—II," in 1906 he opens with a newspaper-style lead as he had his *Round the World* of a quarter century earlier.

Carnegie always wrote of things that had caught or would catch the public eye, and on which he sought to influence his readers.

If we seek a reason for this lack of change, perhaps it is to be found in the time-sequence involved. By the time Carnegie entered the field of magazine writing he had reached maturity, his ideas and habits largely formed. What few changes we find are easily traceable to changes in his own ideas and in the world around him. Anyone arguing against the industrialist's sole responsibility for the ideas and language of the books, articles and other works bearing his name must be hard-put to find anything which could rebut the complete homogeneity of his writings.

CHAPTER 5

Political Pragmatist: 1881-1911

ANDREW Carnegie plunged into political writing as he plunged into everything else—headlong. His first magazine article,[1] instead of being the interested or amused view of British ways that Morley may well have expected, was a slashing attack on the political and social system of the Mother Country. Carnegie was ever a strenuously political man. The basis of his opinions and attitudes may be readily seen in his antecedents and early life.

His family, especially the Morrisons on his mother's side, were nonconformists in religion and Chartist in politics. His home town, Dunfermline, although the ancient seat of Scottish kings, had been one of the principal centers of Chartism. And although the movement's near-revolution was coming to an end at the time the Carnegies removed to America, his formative years had been filled with news and talk of its planning, campaigning, marches, strikes, and even threats of outright revolt.

The Chartist movement, except for the brief insurrection of the "physical force men" at Newport in 1839, was not excessively radical by today's standards, though far out for Britain of its day. The name "Chartist" came from a six-point program, the "People's Charter," which was formulated by the London Workingmen's Association late in 1837. Its aims were: 1. equal electoral areas; 2. universal suffrage; 3. payment of members of Parliament; 4. abolition of property qualifications for voting; 5. voting by ballot; and 6. annual parliaments. Most of these were eventually adopted, several of them by the Reform Bill whose passage was secured by Gladstone nearly half a century afterward, at least partly through Carnegie's agitation during his newspaper period.

In America Carnegie found what to him—individualist that he was—proved the key that opened all doors: the right of every man to full citizenship and the ballot. Even before he was old enough to vote he was bombarding newspaper editors with letters on the abolition of slavery, and soon afterward, opposing secession.

With the move to New York in 1868 and entry into the city's intellectual life, Carnegie discovered evolution and came under the sway of Herbert Spencer, whom he never fully understood and sometimes misquoted. But although he made it his motto that, "All is well, since all grows better," and proudly announced his belief in socialism, it is extremely doubtful whether he at any time really agreed with its tenets. Rather, as Wall ably demonstrates,[2] Carnegie developed a philosophy of his own. It was made up of his early religious and political training, rugged individualism, desire for mastery and achievement, greed, generosity, and a conviction that the world—and especially those close to him—needed his ideas and guidance. No small element was his struggle of conscience over having indulged in what in 1868 he had alluded to as the "worship of the golden calf."

By 1880 his political credo might be described as a benevolent capitalistic individualism in a republican setting. Barring special privilege and inherited wealth, opportunity was within reach of everyone, and affluence could be attained by those with the energy and intelligence to seek it. Poverty was useful in developing manhood ("Adversity makes men, prosperity monsters") but severe suffering from the same source should be alleviated by legislation and both public and private charity.

I Triumphant Democracy

Carnegie's great statement of this belief came in 1886 in *Triumphant Democracy, or Fifty Years' March of the Republic*.[3] It was the best planned and most widely read of his works, except for the magazine article on "Wealth," which appeared in the *North American Review* three years later and was reprinted all over Europe in many languages.[4]

In his *Autobiography*, Carnegie relates the genesis of the work:

My third literary venture, "Triumphant Democracy," had its origin in realizing how little the best-informed foreigner, or even Briton, knew of America, and how distorted that little was. It was prodigious what these eminent Englishmen did not then know about the Republic. My first talk with Mr. Gladstone in 1882 can never be forgotten. When I had occasion to say that the majority of the English-speaking race was now republican, and it was now a minority of monarchists who were upon the defensive, he said:

"Why, how is that?"

"Well, Mr. Gladstone," I said, "the Republic holds sway over a larger number of English-speaking people than the population of Great Britain and all her colonies, even if the English-speaking colonies were numbered twice over."

"Ah! how is that? What is your population?"

"Sixty-six millions, and yours is not much more than half."

"Ah, yes, surprising!"

With regard to the wealth of the nations, it was equally surprising for him to learn that the census of 1880 proved the hundred-year-old Republic could purchase Great Britain and Ireland and all their realized capital and investments and then pay off Britain's debt, and yet not exhaust her fortune. But the most startling statement of all was that which I was able to make when the question of Free Trade was touched upon. I pointed out that America was now the greatest manufacturing nation in the world. . . . I quoted Mulhall's[5] figures: British manufactures in 1880, eight hundred and sixteen millions, sterling; American manufactures eleven hundred and twenty-six millions, sterling. His one word was:

"Incredible!"

Other startling statements followed, and he asked:

"Why does not some writer take up this subject and present the facts in a simple and direct form to the world?"

I was then, as a matter of fact, gathering material for "Triumphant Democracy," in which I intended to perform the very service which he indicated, as I informed him.[6]

Perhaps it was somewhat later that a second reason for the book occurred to Carnegie. In his preface, after setting out "the lamentable ignorance concerning the new land which I have found even in the highest political circles of the old," he adds:

I believed, also, that my attempt would give Americans a better idea of the great work their country has done and is doing in the world. . . . During its progress I have been deeply interested in it, and it may truly be regarded as a labor of love—the tribute of a dutiful and grateful son of an adopted country which has removed the stigma of inferiority which his native land saw proper to impress upon him at birth, and has made him, in the estimation of its great laws as well as in his own estimation (much the more important consideration), the peer of any human being who draws the breath of life, be he pope, kaiser, priest or king . . . a citizen.

II *Theme of the Work*

Having disposed of such preliminaries (probably as an afterthought following the completion of the book) Carnegie opens with an appropriate quotation from Milton, and then roars on—still in his early style learned from the newspapers: "The old nations of the earth creep on at a snail's pace; the Republic thunders past with the rush of an express. The United States, the growth of a single century, has already reached the foremost rank among nations, and is destined to outdistance all others in the race. In population, in wealth, in annual savings, and in public credit; in freedom from debt, in agriculture, and in manufactures, America already leads the civilized world."

The first chapter of the book is titled "The Republic," and in it Carnegie does not delay in supporting his theory that democracy is one of the important reasons for the nation's startling growth. He does not, as he has sometimes been accused of doing, aver that the political system has been the sole reason for such rapid growth. He sets up the three "most important factors in this problem." The first, in keeping with his constant emphasis on the vital nature of heredity, is "the ethnic character of the people";[7] next, the environment, the "topographical and climatic conditions"; and third, "the influence of political institutions founded upon the equality of the citizen."

"The Republic" had faced two great dangers, human slavery, and "the millions of foreigners who came from all lands to the hospitable shores of the nation, many of them ignorant of the English language, and all unaccustomed to the exercise of political duties." The first had been voided by emancipation and giving full citizenship rights to the former slaves. The second had been changed into a benefit by:

> The generosity . . . with which the Republic has dealt with these [immigrant] people. They are won to her side by being offered for their *subject*ship the boon of citizenship. For denial of equal privileges at home, the new land meets them with perfect equality, saying, be not only with us, but be of us. They reach the shores of the Republic *subjects* (insulting word), and she makes them citizens; serfs and she makes them men, and their children she takes gently by the hand and leads to the public schools which she has founded for her own children, and gives them, without money and without price, a good primary education as the most precious gift which she has, even in her bountiful hand, to bestow upon human beings. This is Democracy's "gift of welcome" to the new comer. The poor immigrant can not help growing up passionately fond of his new home . . . and thus the threatened danger is averted—the homogeneity of the people secured.[8]

This, in Carnegie's view, was the key to America's greatness and rapid growth. Other nations of similar blood and equally helpful environment might fail of achievement because of internal strife, ignorance, and lack of individual opportunity. "The Republic" was going forward as the Social Darwinian credo envisioned it should. All was well, and all growing better.

III   *Structure of the Book*

Having set up his thesis, Carnegie proceeds to elaborate it to some extent, but principally in regard to its results. He evidently considers his point proved by his logic, but even more certainly by his statistics. Perhaps in the back of his mind were the religious teachings of his youth,[9] such as "By their fruits ye shall know them,"[10] or "Show me your faith without your works, and I will show you my faith by my works."[11]

The main body of *Triumphant Democracy* includes four undesignated sections: The American people and their lives, Chapters II–VIII; the nation's material progress, Chapters IX–XIII; its cultural advancement, Chapters XIV–XV; and its government, Chapters XVI–XIX. The final chapter serves as a conclusion.

Opening the section on the American people, Carnegie expands and elaborates on the subject as introduced in the first chapter, using numerous statistics. The white American (he conveniently omits the black element until late in the chapter) is still, as of 1880, four-fifths British, the remainder largely German and French. This admixture has proved a helpful one, providing more imagination and softening the grim harshness of "those island mastiffs": "Toleration in the Briton is truly admirable; the leading Radical and the leading Tory-Democrat are found dining together.... Well, the American is even more tolerant.... Once in four years he warms up and takes sides, opposing hosts confront each other and a stranger would naturally think that only violence could result whichever side won. The morning after the election his arm is upon his opponent's shoulder and they are chaffing each other" (29–30).

Far from being opposed to immigration, Carnegie considers it one of the most helpful factors in expanding the country. It is usually the best who are dissatisfied in old lands. The new arrivals are a minority; with all that have come, America's population is still seven-eighths native-born. And he shrewdly predicts that "At these rates of advance the 'Wild West' is rapidly becoming a thing of the past, and in a few years it will be a thickly settled land" (39). Even the apprehensions that idleness and trouble-making would develop among the slaves freed by the Civil War have proved groundless, he finds.

Turning to the growth of cities and towns, Carnegie keeps the reader's head swimming with facts and figures which show how municipalities have mushroomed almost overnight, without perceptible diminution of the agrarian population. But America has no reason to fear such growth, since it is the result of economic laws. Here his devotion to Spencer breaks out: "Oh, these grand, immutable, all-wise laws of natural forces, how perfectly they work if human legislators would only let them alone!" (48). And from time to time Carnegie reverts to favorite themes of his more casual writing, with quotations from classical and popular authors, references to chance (after recounting the story of the man who could have bought the site of Chicago for a pair of boots, but didn't have them: "How many chances in life do we miss just for the want of the boots. Moral: Get the boots" [53]), and love of the fatherland. He contrasts the slow early growth of Boston—by implication because it was then under monarchy—with newer areas, and concludes with a peroration he might have delivered from the platform: "When the people reign in the old home as they do in the new, the two nations will be one people, and the bonds which unite them the world combined shall not break asunder. They clasp hands. Democracy cries to democracy, 'We stand for the rights of man, the day of kings and peers is past.' . . . No peal so grand as that, save one, that which proclaims the substitution of peaceful arbitration for war the world over. . . . Democracy goes marching on" (72–73).

Carnegie devotes thirty-five pages to describing the improvement of living conditions, especially in small towns and rural areas during the previous half century, contrasting them with such areas in Britain, and closely relating the benefits to universal suffrage. The chapter on "Occupations" is a survey to provide background, with little definite relation to the thesis of the book.

Despite his faith in education, Carnegie's chapter on that subject is largely a matter of statistics, with few comparisons to education in Britain until almost the end. At that point he lists leading colleges and universities endowed by private funds, noting the rarity of such a practice in Britain. His enthusiasm breaks out in a Biblical paraphrase: "The moral to be drawn from America by every nation is this: "Seek ye first the education of the people and all other political blessings will be added unto you" (150).

The chapter on "Religion" is largely devoted to statistics showing that America, with complete freedom, had a larger proportion of active church members than Britain, and that most denominations were better supported than even the established churches of the mother country. Concluding with "Pauperism and Crime," Carnegie notes that much of this was among those newly arrived in America and unable to find and hold jobs, and cites the close relationship between crime and poverty: "America exhibits not only the least poverty, but the best system of alleviating it" (171). Things are improving. "The next generation, or the next beyond, will probably read with horror of our inflicting the death punishment upon human beings." Many states have already abolished the death penalty. "Judged by this standard, the Democracy stands the test well" (178-79).

IV *Material Progress*

Five chapters, totaling about 130 pages, describe the progress of America in agriculture, manufacturing, mining (including oil), commerce, and transportation. Except for an undercurrent of boasting that in most of these achievements the new land far outstrips the Old World, the chapters contain little of note except statistics, interestingly presented. "Trade and Commerce" includes several pages of discussion on tariff, upholding the position of the United States, particularly against those of France and England. Each chapter ends with a few inspirational words on peace or democracy, the paragraph closing the chapter on "Railways and Waterways" serving as peroration for the whole section: "We have not travelled far yet, with all our progress upon the upward path, but we still go marching on. That which is is better than that which has been. It is the mission of Democracy to lead in this triumphant march and improve step by step the conditions under which the masses live; to ring out the Old, and to ring in the New; and in this great work the Republic rightly leads the van" (315).

V *Cultural Factors*

Carnegie's two chapters on cultural progress are notable not so much for their content as that they were included in the work at all. Few leading industrialists of the day in America would have even thought of the subject. For the most part, industrial heads were still men who had grown up in the mills, and whose schooling in many instances was not significantly better than the few years which the "white haired Scotch devil" had been able to secure before going to work at thirteen.

The fact that Carnegie gives less than fifty pages to the two chapters might indicate that he knew his side was still badly out-matched in such a contest. America was just beginning to come into its own in almost every field of cultural endeavor. What showing could he make in a contest on poetry with only Poe, Bryant, Bret Harte, and a few others to match against such giants as Browning, Scott, Byron, Wordsworth, Keats, Shelley, and a host of others Britain had produced in the same period?

Ever the canny fighter, Carnegie completely ignores such an unequal contest, and launches a flank attack. First he quotes some writers who had denigrated American art and music of the period, particularly singling out "a writer of about the same time, in the London *Quarterly Review*" who had stated that "a high and refined genius for art is indigenous to monarchies, and under such a form of government alone can it flourish, either vigorously or securely. The United States of North America can never expect to possess a fine school of art, so long as they retain their present system" (318–19).

"Art indigenous to monarchies!" Carnegie thunders. "Did anyone ever hear such an absurdity? The great law is that each shall produce fruit after its kind, but this genius makes a monarchy produce the greatest of all republics, the republic of art." He supports the argument:

> Who knows or cares who Michelangelo's father was; or what was Beethoven's birth, or whether Raphael was an aristocrat, or Wagner the son of a poor actuary of police? Just imagine monarchy in art— a hereditary painter, for instance, or a sculptor who only was his father's son, or a musician, because born in the profession! . . .
> This curious writer, who would have monarchy allied with art, built his theory upon the exploded idea that only monarchs and the aristocracy, which flutters around courts, could or would patronize the beautiful. That theory is unfortunate, in view of the fact that the best patrons of art are the Americans. (318–21)

He goes on to cite the growing number of art groups and museums in the United States, and the constant flow of works of art to this country. The American "is recognized now as one of the shrewdest, as well as one of the most liberal buyers." At an auction "he is no mean competitor, for he carries a pocket full of dollars, and is not afraid to spend them where he is sure of getting his money's worth" (325).

As to architecture and music, he offers similar arguments, particularly citing the great numbers of theaters and opera houses in the United States, even in small towns. From a trade guide he picks out, among others, "Centralia: . . . Population one thousand five hundred," with a theater and an opera house, and Oshkosh, "away out in Wisconsin, two hundred miles from Chicago, with a population of twenty-two thousand," which showed three theaters, one the "New Opera House. Stage, forty-two by seventy feet; seats one thousand one hundred" (335).

Turning to literature, Carnegie stresses the astonishing growth of newspapers, splendid progress in the magazine field—citing *Harper's Magazine* and *Century* in particular, and in the juvenile field *St. Nicholas* and *Harper's Young People*—and the heavy sale of encyclopedias, as well as the large and increasing number of public libraries. "Triumphant Democracy is triumphant in nothing more than in this, [he concludes] that her members are readers and buyers of books and reading matter beyond the members of any government of a class, but in this particular each system is only seen to be true to its nature. The monarchist boasts more bayonets, the republican more books" (363).

VI *Government*

Finally offering an explanation of the triumphant democracy about which he has been boasting, Carnegie opens "The Federal Constellation" with the key quotation from the *Declaration of Independence*: "We hold these truths to be self-evident that all men are created free and (*sic*) equal, and are endowed by their Creator with certain inalienable rights, among which (*sic*) are life, liberty, and the pursuit of happiness" (365).[12] "Round this doctrine of the Declaration of Independence as its central sun," he continues, "the constellation of states revolves. The equality of the citizen is decreed by the fundamental law. All acts, all institutions, are based upon this idea. There is not one shred of privilege, hence no classes. . . . The President has not a shred of privilege which is not the birthright of every other citizen. The people are not levelled down, but levelled up to the full dignity of equal citizenship beyond which no man can go." This, he avers, instead of creating a "dead level of uniformity," gives leeway for the operation of natural laws. Primogeniture and entail are unknown, and "There are but three generations in America from shirt sleeves to shirt sleeves" (364–66).[13]

He goes on to characterize the rights of states as "home rule," and describes principal features of the federal government, beginning with the Supreme Court, and continuing with the Legislative Department (*sic*), principally the Senate. After listing among the powers of the latter those which relate to making war and concluding treaties, he warns:

My American readers may not be aware of the fact that, while in Britain an act of Parliament is necessary before works for a supply of water or a mile of railway can be constructed, six or seven men can plunge the nation into war, or, what is perhaps equally disastrous, commit it to entangling alliances wthout consulting Parliament at all. This is the most pernicious effect flowing from the monarchical theory, for these men do this in "the king's name," who is in theory still a real monarch, although in reality only a convenient puppet, to be used by the cabinet at pleasure to suit their own ends. (380–81)

He concludes the chapter with a discussion of the presidency and praise of the Constitution.

"The Government's Non-political Work," except for its first and final nine pages, is not written by Carnegie. He had planned, he explains, to visit Washington and write an account of the various bureaus, but could not spare the time. "The happy thought occurred to me to send my secretary, Mr. [James H.] Bridge, to perform the task, with a request to write up the subject and see what he could make of it. He has done so well that I cannot do better than incorporate his account" (414–15).

There follows a twenty-two-page account in a style evidently attempting to approximate Carnegie's, but completely lacking his frequent use of "I." Following this Carnegie continues with some state and municipal functions, a description of the Sanitary Commission's work during the Civil War, and a page or so on the Centennial of 1876. "We can confidently claim for the Democracy that it produces a people self-reliant beyond all others. . . . The monarchical form lacks the vigor and elasticity to cope with the republican in any department of government whatever" (445).

The chapter on "The National Balance Sheet" offers a comparison of American and British budgets, deprecating the high cost of monarchy and hereditary privilege.

In the final chapter, "General Reflections," Carnegie points out that American stability is due to two factors: no one desires any change in fundamental laws, and regular elections provide a convenient way to get rid of undesirable office holders. To a considerable extent this chapter parallels the article "As Others See Us," closing with a hope for a reunion when Britain becomes a democracy.

VII *Characteristics*

In style, language, and opinions, *Triumphant Democracy* is close to the spirit and attitudes of Carnegie's articles, speeches, and letters of the same period—one of transition from Social Darwinism to a somewhat paternal capitalism. It is much more involved with statistics than any of his other works, as would appear necessary from the approach he adopted. For much the same reason it introduces fewer personal experiences, and literary references are less frequent, although appearing, when used, in his typically careless style, given from memory, often incorrect and almost never identified.

His use of humor is about the same as in his other works, not frequent, but sometimes with good effect. A fair example is "When the fair young American asked the latest lordling who did her country the honor to visit it, how the aristocratic leisure classes spent their time, he replied: 'Oh, they go from one house to another, don't you know, and enjoy themselves, you know. They never do any work, you know.' 'Oh,' she replied, 'we have such people too—tramps'" (130).

Although Carnegie occasionally admits some of the difficulties and darker spots of America, the work does in general warrant the criticism given it at the time of publication that it was all sweetness and light. Nor can this all be justified by his reply to George William Curtis's question, "Where are the shadows?" His answer was: "The book was written at high noon, when the sun casts no shadows."[14]

Triumphant Democracy is gaudy, from phraseology to Carnegie's personally designed red cover with quotations from Gladstone and Salisbury, an erect gold pyramid for "Republic," and a reversed one for "Monarchy," and on the spine a crown, upside down. But he wrote in a gaudy era. In his Preface, after telling of the labor of gathering facts, he adds that the question came to him: "Shall these dry bones live?" So he "tried to coat the wholesome medicine of facts in the sweetest and purest sugar of fancy at my command." And, as Wall rightly observes: "Curiously enough, the 'dry bones' do live, for the book is filled with anecdotes, editorial comment, and, above all, Carnegie's own ebullient personality"[15]

VIII *Who Wrote* Triumphant Democracy?

Some years ago the authenticity of Carnegie's writing—particularly *Triumphant Democracy*—came under attack, principally by Fritz Redlich in a review of R. G. McCloskey's *American Conservatism in the Age of Enterprise: A Study of William Graham Sumner, Stephen J. Field and Andrew Carnegie*.[16] His criticism reads, in part:

> The question is easily formulated: can the researcher working on businessmen's minds legitimately base his investigations on their published writings? The question must be answered in the negative unless the student concerned can prove the businessman in question really wrote what was published under his name. Or to put it differently, when a wealthy and powerful American business leader "writes" a book or pamphlet, the assumption is that he hired a ghost writer.
>
> In the case of Carnegie we know (at least for the period in which *Triumphant Democracy* was written) who the ghost writer was ... James Howard Bridge had been Herbert Spencer's secretary from 1879 to 1884. In the latter year he came to the United States, where he became Carnegie's "literary assistant,"[17] resigning from that position in 1889. How much he contributed to the *Forum* essays of 1886 and to *Triumphant Democracy*, and in turn how great was Carnegie's share therein is not known to the reviewer, nor does he

know who Carnegie's later "literary assistants," were. . . . In this case the line runs from Spencer to Bridge, then to Bridge plus Carnegie. . . .

Bridge . . . may have had a more than fifty per cent share in the book, and a considerable influence on Carnegie's thinking, the latter thereby absorbing Spencerism.

This statement ignores important factors that completely vitiate Redlich's argument. 1. It was not customary in 1886 for leading industrialists to write books, or to employ ghost writers. Carnegie may well be called the first important writing industrialist. 2. Bridge was Carnegie's secretary, not an editorial assistant. Internal evidence would indicate that the "almost indispensable aid" for which Carnegie credits his "clever secretary, Mr. Bridge" (vii) was largely in gathering and arranging material. 3. The only part of *Triumphant Democracy* which Bridge wrote—and for this he received full credit—was part of one chapter, Chapter XVIII. 4. The line certainly did not run "from Spencer to Bridge, then to Bridge plus Carnegie." From 1870 (when Bridge was but fourteen years of age) Carnegie was an announced Spencerian, and by 1882 he and Spencer were close friends. 5. From his youth Carnegie had been an avid writer. His writing habits (on a pad with a stub pencil) are well known from outside evidence, as are his statements of the pleasure that he enjoyed in such work. And in the winter of 1881–82 he had written in a book for his friends and later retained when it was revised for general circulation: "If any man wants *bona fide* substantial power and influence in this world, he must handle the pen. That's flat. Truly it is a nobler weapon than the sword, and a much nobler one than the tongue, both of which have nearly had their day."[18] 6. It is utterly unbelievable that a man so personally opinionated as Carnegie, and so jealous of reputation, would have permitted his name to be used with something written by an employee, with which he might not agree. 7. The style and opinions of *Triumphant Democracy* are quite in agreement with those of his other books, articles, speeches, and letters.[19] The style of Bridge's part chapter is readily distinguishable, despite an obvious effort to agree with Carnegie's own. In fact, the Carnegian touches in this section may well have been inserted by the book's author, rather than the other way around.

IX *The Revised Edition*

Triumphant Democracy was a highly successful book in the United States, where it went through four printings and sold more than 30,000 copies. In Britain it did almost equally well, besides having a cheap edition in paperback which sold an additional 40,000. It was translated into several languages, and sold all over Europe.

To say that it created a sensation is an understatement. But not all the reaction was approving. The *Saturday Review*, for instance, denounced both the writing and the logic, and called Carnegie a snob for saying that being inferior to peers and monarch was degrading to a man.[20] And a grand jury at Wolverhampton found that a reference to the Royal family constituted a "scandalous, abominable and treasonous libel," and recommended prosecuting Carnegie and taking his book off the shelves of the Free Library.[21]

Delighted rather than discouraged by the furor, Carnegie completely revised the book following the 1890 census, with the new subtitle "Sixty Years' March of the Republic."[22] He opened the Preface with an account of Curtis's criticism[23] and his reply, adding, "Of course, everything in the Republic is not perfect. But neither is everything perfect in any land, or even in the sun. We are continually reminded that even that glorious luminare has its spots.... This book is not intended either to describe or dilate upon the spots upon our national sun.... The scope of this book is to show what we have to be thankful for, and not what we have to lament, as compared with other aggregations of the human race elsewhere."

Significantly, he omits the credit to Bridge, with whom he had quarreled in 1889, and to J. D. Champlin, Jr., of Scribner's. He expressed appreciation to four others, including a Columbia University professor and the superintendent and assistant superintendent of the census. Besides updating census data to the 1890 figures, Carnegie adapted or rewrote every chapter, including Bridge's work, which he used without giving credit.

Perhaps he was being crass and bitter over their quarrel. But Carnegie was seldom a man to hold any grudge long, and he may have withheld the name because of the task of explaining the changes. Considerable parts were omitted, including all Carnegie's original ten pages of the chapter; and he added a little more than enough to keep the length about equal to Bridge's original contribution.

The plan of the book was largely retained, but two of the sections were expanded, and the order of the second and third was reversed, apparently to give cultural progress precedence over material change. Carnegie also switched the order of the first two governmental chapters, bringing foreign affairs more to the forefront. And in place of the final observations he added two chapters—"The Record of the Decade—1880–1890," and "A Look Ahead."

Although every chapter is updated, trimmed, recast, and in most cases improved, few of the changes are radical. In the first section Carnegie has added as Chapter VI, "Wages and the Cost of Living," closely related to an article he contributed about the same time to *Contemporary Review* (September 1894) on "The Cost of Living in Britain Compared with the United States," and reprinted later in his *The Empire of Business*. The two chapters on cultural matters are expanded and made into four by separating literature, painting and sculpture, music and architecture, but without essentially altering the approach or arguments. In some cases Carnegie's more startling attacks on the British monarchy have been somewhat toned down. Except perhaps in this respect, the changes do not appear to reflect any variations in the author's thinking.

"The Record of the Decade" is a rather lively account of American progress between 1880 and 1890—and in part between 1860 and 1890, frequently compared with similar figures for Britain. In "A Look Ahead," which was published in *North American Review* a short time after the new edition appeared in book form, Carnegie reviews relations between the two countries from the time of their separation, showing a gradual and increasingly fast improvement. He closes with a stirring, yet touching vision of reunion within a fairly short time, concluding, "Let men say what they will, therefore, I say that as surely as the sun in the heavens once shone upon Britain and America united, so is it one morning to rise, shine upon, and greet again 'The Reunited States,' 'The British-American Union.'"

Although perhaps a better work than the first, the second *Triumphant Democracy* is heavier reading than its predecessor, and had a far lower sale.

X *Other Political Writings*

The next most important collection of political writings by Andrew Carnegie appears in the latter half of *The Gospel of Wealth*,[24] a collection of twelve previously published articles and one address (which had been printed in the *Scottish Leader*). The first six chapters (he joined the second and third articles), were on economics, the latter six political. These included four on foreign affairs, and two on the mechanics of government.

Earliest of these in time, but third in order is "Democracy in England," which had originally appeared in *North American Review* for January 1886, just before the publication of *Triumphant Democracy*. Celebrating the passage of Gladstone's Reform Bills of 1884 and 1885, which provided almost universal suffrage and near-equality of representation in Britain, it comments on the results of the first election, discusses problems which may be expected to arise, and predicts that the country will fully adopt the democratic system within two decades. Immediately following is the speech, *Home Rule in America*, delivered in Glasgow in September 1887, and printed the same month. In it Carnegie discusses the American system of government in much the same way and with some of the materials used in *Triumphant Democracy*. The latter half is given to the Irish problem, to which he felt the proper answer was home rule—that is, a system like the powers of the states in the Union.

"Imperial Federation," published in *Nineteenth Century* for September 1891, is representative of a number of similar articles Carnegie wrote about this period in regard to tariffs. It was inspired by the sentiment for special trade concessions within the empire, partly in retaliation against the McKinley Tariff Act of 1890, which was sharply protective. Originally favoring free trade, especially when his mills could produce iron and steel more cheaply than those of the mother country, Carnegie had gradually come around to a position favoring free trade for England, which produced many manufactures, but little food, while for America, with its overproduction in agriculture, there should be a tariff on manufactured articles.

The two most important political articles in the collection are "Distant Possessions" and "Americanism Versus Imperialism," published in *North American Review* immediately following the Spanish-American War. Carnegie had relaxed his peace principles at the time of the conflict, on the ground that it was justified in order to give independence to Cuba. But he was horrified when the United States took over the Philippines and other island possessions at its conclusion. He became a crusader against imperialism, and especially in these articles pointed out the dangers of dependencies, citing England's problems with India and other possessions. Particularly in the earlier one, Carnegie exhibits some of his best and most persuasive writing:

If it be a noble aspiration for the . . . Cuban, as it was for the citizen of the United States himself, and for the various South American republics once under Spain, to have a country to live and, if necessary, to die for, why is not the revolt noble which the man of the Philippines has been making against Spain? Is it possible that the Republic is to be placed in the position of the suppressor of the Philippine struggle for independence? Surely, that is impossible. With what faces shall we hang in the school-houses of the Philippines our own Declaration of Independence, and yet deny independence to them? What response will the heart of the Philippine Islander make as he reads of Lincoln's Emancipation Proclamation? Are we to practice independence and preach subordination, to teach rebellion in our books, yet to stamp it out with our swords, to sow seed of revolt and expect the harvest of loyalty?[25]

CHAPTER 6

Free-Wheeling Economist: 1883-1916

BY far the most famous work by Andrew Carnegie was not really a book, but a collection of his magazine articles, along with one speech. "Wealth" had appeared in two parts in the *North American Review* in 1889, and had been reprinted in several languages in magazines and pamphlet form, for almost eleven years before *The Gospel of Wealth* was published. But as a book it made an immense impression, and went into a second edition the following year.

Although the second half of the volume was concerned largely with political questions, it was the first half dealing with economics, which proved sensational. And the important part of this dealt with unequal distribution of wealth. Carnegie had long been concerned with this vexing problem, and offered an unusual and eye-catching twist to a partial solution which he had previously advocated, and which had been suggested by others, going back as far as Tom Paine. More than a century earlier, Paine had suggested breaking up huge fortunes by heavy inheritance taxes. Carnegie agreed, but held up an ideal—that the right-minded plutocrat should not wait until death to do good with his money; to be sure it went for the desired ends, he should give it away during his lifetime.

Even this was far from new in Carnegie's thought. Two decades before writing the key article which gave the book its name, he had put down a memo embodying the plan for even a fairly modest income.[1] And two years before the publication, he had told Gladstone he "should consider it a disgrace to die a rich man."[2]

Although his father had left the Presbyterian Church, Carnegie had been surrounded in his boyhood by strong Calvinist influences, that "Protestant ethic" with its emphasis on work, the duty of thrift, and the right to private property because it could be used in the divine service. His Chartist upbringing may have caused him to lean towards socialism, but only in theory, not practice. Nor did his Darwinian Socialism, to which he seems never to have paid much more than lip service, cause him to oppose some legal intervention, as well as private charity, to relieve human need. Well versed in the Bible, he adopted many Judeo-Christian principles, though rejecting the theological content.

The basis of his economic system was *The Wealth of Nations* by Adam Smith, whom he greatly admired as a thinker and fellow-Scot.[3] He was influenced on the tariff by Henry C. Carey, and later quoted favorably from John Stuart Mill's *Principles of Political Economy* when he shocked the nation by coming out in 1908 for free trade.[4] Nine months earlier his address, *The Worst Banking System in the World*, before the Economics Club of New York, had been published in *The Outlook*.[5] It was highly praised, and Carnegie had more than seventy thousand copies printed and sent to every legislator and banker in the country. The address is credited with helping stimulate the discussion which eventually resulted in the Federal Reserve System.[6] Despite his close friendship with John Bright, Carnegie blasted the doctrines of the Manchester School in an article in *Nineteenth Century*.[7]

I *The Opening Gun*

But nothing else in all Carnegie's economic writing ever created such a sensation as a pair of articles titled simply "Wealth" and "The Best Fields for Philanthropy" in the June and December issues of *North American Review* in 1889. Whatever was lacking was supplied by W. T. Stead, who titled the first article "The Gospel of Wealth" when given permission to reprint it in his *Pall Mall Gazette*. From there it was widely reprinted in several languages.

In the second article Carnegie relates the dramatic circumstances connected with the publication of the first: "The manuscript reached [*North American* editor Allen Thorndike Rice] in the morning, and late in the evening of the same day he called to say that it pleased him so much that he had determined to publish it in the forthcoming number, instead of holding it for the succeeding issue, as had been intended. . . . Sitting in my library, Mr. Rice expressed a wish to hear the author read his manuscript. I read and he listened from beginning to end, making but one interruption."[8]

By 1889 Carnegie had passed the stage in his writing where he felt called upon to use a fiery opening, in the newspaper style of his times. He begins "Wealth" quietly, but at the very crux of the problem to which it is addressed: "The problem of our age is the proper administration of wealth, that the ties of brotherhood may still bind together the rich and poor in harmonious relationship." Without breaking the paragraph, he approaches the problem first from a historical standpoint. True to his early training he equated capitalism with civilization, and followed Darwin on what is best for the race. In former days, as with Indians of his day, there was little difference between the living standard of the chief and his poorest brave. "The contrast between the palace of the millionaire and the cottage of the laborer with us today measures the change which has come with civilization. This change, however, is not to be deplored, but welcomed as highly beneficial. It is well, nay, essential, for the progress of the race that the houses of some should be homes for all that is highest and best in literature and the arts, and for all the refinements of civilization, rather than that none should be so. Much better this great irregularity than universal squalor. Without wealth there can be no Maecenas."[9]

A "relapse" to old conditions "would sweep away civilization with it." Carnegie continues, "But, whether the change be for good or ill, it is upon us, beyond our power to alter, and therefore, to be accepted and made the best of. It is a waste of time to criticize the inevitable" (2).

Carnegie then proceeds to trace the rise of manufacturing, and praises the result that "The poor enjoy what the rich could not before afford. What were luxuries have become the necessaries." He does not discount the social cost involved, but considers it—as well he might—both worthwhile and unavoidable. Here is the very basis of his creed as a capitalist, as well as of his "Gospel of Wealth":

The price we pay for this salutary change is, no doubt, great. We assemble thousands of operatives in the factory, and in the mine, of whom the employer can know little or nothing, and to whom he is little better than a myth. All intercourse between them is at an end. Rigid castes are formed, and, as usual, mutual ignorance breeds mutual distrust. Each caste is without sympathy with the other, and ready to credit anything disparaging in regard to it. Under the law of competition, the employer of thousands is forced into the strictest economies, among which the rates paid to labor figure prominently, and often there is friction between the employer and the employed, between capital and labor, between rich and poor. Human society loses homogeneity.

The price which society pays for the law of competition, like the price it pays for cheap comforts and luxuries, is also great; but the advantages of this law are also greater than its cost—for it is to this law that we owe our wonderful material development, which brings improved conditions in its train. But whether the law be benign or not, we must say of it, as we say of the change in the conditions of men, to which we have referred: It is here; we cannot evade it; no substitutes for it have been found; and while the law may be some-times hard for the individual, it is best for the race, because it insures the survival of the fittest in every department. (3–4)

Soon Carnegie launches into an attack on any other systems. They are not in order "because the condition of the race is better than it has been with any other which has been tried." The effect of new substitutes is uncertain. Socialism and anarchy are attacking the foundations of civilization, because it began when "the capable, industrious workman said to his incompe-tent and lazy fellow, 'If thou dost not sow, thou shalt not reap'" (5–6).

At this point Carnegie really arrives at the main question: what is the proper mode of administering wealth? He feels and says that he has the only true solution: "There are but three modes in which surplus wealth can be disposed of. It can be left to the families of the decedents; or it can be bequeathed for public purposes; or, finally, it can be administered by its possessors during their lives" (8). With a severity possibly born of his own early privation and amply supported from the antics of wealthy scions of Pittsburgh and New York families, Carnegie warns of the personal and national dangers of large inheritances.

The second mode "is only a means for the disposal of wealth, provided a man is content to wait until he is dead before he becomes of much good in the world." There are many ways, however, in which the intention of a man who leaves money for public purposes may be thwarted, or the money wasted. Carnegie roguishly concludes: "Besides this, it may fairly be said that no man is to be extolled for doing what he cannot help doing, nor is he to be thanked by the community to which he only leaves wealth at death. Men who leave vast sums in this way may fairly be thought men who would not have left it at all had they been able to take it with them" (10–11).

As an alternative, Carnegie points to inheritance taxes, and urges a graduated tax, which he claims will do more good than many "trifling amounts" scattered among individuals. He cites the Cooper Institute, and hopes "[William T. Tilden's] $5 million bequest for a free library in New York may do good. But it would have been better for him to use the money while still alive." He asserts: "This, then, is held to be the duty of the man of wealth: To set an example of modest, unostentatious living, shunning display or extravagance; to provide moderately for the legitimate wants of those dependent upon him; and, after doing so, to consider all surplus revenues which come to him simply as trust funds, which he is called upon to administer, and strictly bound as a matter of duty to administer in a manner which, in his judgment, is best calculated to produce the most beneficial results for the community" (15).

Reviews of *The Gospel of Wealth* commented that the author found it "as impossible to name exact amounts or actions as it is to define good manners, good taste, or the rules of propriety."[10] Few if any suggested that it might have been ridiculous for him to name an amount that would sustain his own lavish living, or a limit of ostentation that would give approval to his castle in Scotland, with its retinue of servants and a bagpiper to wake the household for breakfast.

In the original draft of his manuscript, Carnegie had warned against giving so as to encourage "the slothful, the drunken, the unworthy," adding: "Of every thousand dollars spent in so-called charity today, it is probable that nine hundred dollars is unwisely spent—so spent, indeed, as to produce the very evils which it hopes to mitigate or cure." When he was reading the article to Rice, the editor interrupted at this point. "Make it $950," he suggested. And that is the way the passage appeared.[11]

"Thus is the problem of rich and poor to be solved," Carnegie concludes. "The laws of accumulation will be left free, the laws of distribution free. Individualism will continue, but the millionaire will be but a trustee for the poor . . . administering [wealth] for the community far better than it could or would have done for itself. . . . The day is not far distant when the man who dies leaving behind him millions of available wealth, which was free for him to administer during life, will pass away 'unwept, unhonored and unsung,' no matter to what uses he leaves the dross which he cannot take with him. Of such as these the public verdict will then be: 'The man who dies thus rich, dies disgraced.' Such, in my opinion, is the true gospel concerning wealth . . ." (15–19).

It is a typical late-Victorian essay, complete with all the trappings: the masses do not deserve money because they are unable to use it wisely; those who have made money know how to use it and what is best for the poor; property is equated with civilization, success with goodness. What is new is the interesting presentation, along with the earth-shaking idea that a rich man ought to give away his fortune while he is alive, day by day, as he gets more than he needs—something Carnegie himself was still practicing rather gingerly. And it is buttressed by two eye-catching and glittering phrases—"The gospel concerning wealth," and "The man who dies rich dies disgraced" (19).

II Teaching Philanthropy

In December (1889) Carnegie, happy in the international stir the article had created, had contributed a follow-up, also to the *North American Review*, to explain to his fellow millionaires how to perform the duty he had urged on them. In the book he annexes it (with minor changes) to the first. Following the same thinking as before in regard to the masses, he now urges that the man who makes more millions knows better what to do with the surplus than the men who make fewer.

The article was titled "The Best Fields for Philanthropy," and opens with a defense against an attack on the earlier one. The *Pall Mall Gazette*, in a typical British comment, had said, "Great fortunes, says Mr. Carnegie, are great blessings to a community, because such and such things may be done with them. Well, but they are also a great curse, for such and such things are done with them. . . . The 'Gospel of Wealth' is killed by the acts."[12] Carnegie's very sensible reply is that the gospel of Christianity was also killed by the acts. It is no argument against a gospel that it is not lived up to, or against a law that it is broken.

Then turning to his subject, Carnegie observes that, negatively, the first requisite for a really good use of wealth is to take care that a gift shall not have a degrading, pauperizing tendency upon its recipients, and preaches further on the point. Then, positively, he lists what he considers the best uses:

1. For those who can afford very large sums, to found universities.
2. Free libraries and museums.
3. The founding or extension of hospitals, medical colleges, laboratories and similar institutions.
4. Public parks.
5. Meeting and concert halls.
6. Swimming baths.
7. Churches. (26–41)

He suggests, in addition, a wide range of unstated smaller benefactions, suited for those who cannot give large sums. He concludes, "The gospel of wealth but echoes Christ's words. It calls upon the millionaire to sell all that he hath and give it in the highest and best form to the poor. . . . So doing, he will approach his end no longer the ignoble hoarder of useless millions; poor, very poor indeed, in money, but rich, very rich, twenty times a millionaire still, in the affection . . . of his fellow-men. . . . This much is sure: against such riches as these no bars will be found at the gates of Paradise" (43–44).

III *The "Gospel" in Book Form*

Only a few months before selling out his business and retiring, Carnegie gathered thirteen of his published works, seven on economics[13] and the rest on political science, under the title *The Gospel of Wealth*, making only minor changes except for the omission of the introduction to the third article and merging it in the title chapter. As an introduction to the book he used "How I Served My Apprenticeship," an adaptation of the early portion of his autobiography which had been published in *Youth's Companion*, April 23, 1896, including the discredited story about his meeting with Woodruff, still unchanged.[14]

Several of the articles on economics are significant to Carnegie's basic position. "The Advantages of Poverty," from *Nineteenth Century*, March 1891, is an answer to criticisms in that magazine of the original "Wealth": one by Gladstone, who had praised the essay, except for its strictures against inherited wealth,[15] and Hugh Price Hughes, a Methodist divine, who had bitterly attacked it a month later in a symposium which included Archbishop Henry L. Manning and Hermann Adler, Britain's chief rabbi.[16] Hughes, asserting that "as a representative of a particular class of millionaires...[Carnegie] is an anti-Christian phenomenon, a social monstrosity, and a grave political peril," had criticized the essay because it dealt with the administration of wealth, but not the real problem, its distribution. Carnegie's reply, not very forcible or convincing, repeats much of what was in the original two essays on wealth, and introduces his pet themes—the influence of the saintly, hard-working mother (61, 63–64); how poor boys tend to be achievers (64); and—at great length—the dangers of promoting idleness and laziness by impetuous giving (68–71).

"Popular Illusions about Trusts"[17] does not openly defend these monopolies, but holds up to ridicule any effort for laws against them. Large concentrations of capital are necessary for modern industry, and are good, because they increase efficiency. Because of the law of competition, "every attempt to monopolize the manufacture of any staple article carries within its bosom the seeds of failure. Long before we could legislate with

much effect against trusts there would be no necessity for legislation. . . . There should be nothing but encouragement for these
vast aggregations of capital" (101). Though the price may go
up briefly, the article affected will soon become cheaper than
before. "Generally speaking, the advance in prices would have
taken place even if no trusts existed, being caused by increased
demand" (99–100). Carnegie is still relying on his Spencerian
principles: "The great natural laws, being the outgrowth of
human nature and human needs, keep on their irresistible
course" (102).

"An Employer's View of the Labor Question" and "Results
of the Labor Struggle" were originally printed in the April and
August (1886) issues of the *Forum*; the former written just
before, the latter just after, the labor disturbances of 1886.

The former is mostly sweetness and light. Historically viewed,
things are quite hopeful, although the new employer-employee
relation system has not yet evolved. Profit-sharing is a hopeful possibility, as is arbitration of differences, but profit-sharing
is still far off: "The right of the working-man to combine and
to form trades-unions is no less sacred than the right of the
manufacturer to enter into associations and conferences with his
fellows, and it must sooner or later be conceded" (114). Carnegie finally sets up four principles:

First. That compensation be paid the men based upon a sliding
scale in proportion to the prices received for the product.
Second. A proper organization of the men of every works to be
made, by which the natural leaders, the best men, will eventually
come to the front and confer freely with the employers.
Third. Peaceful arbitration to be in all cases resorted to for the
settlement of differences which the owners and the mill committee
cannot themselves adjust.
Fourth. No interruption ever to occur in the operations. . . . (122)

Before the first article was in print, a rash of difficulties
broke out, including scattered violence. The second article,
"Results of the Labor Struggle," is written to provide reasons
and explain results. In it, Carnegie differentiates between the
two major outbursts. At St. Louis a leader of the Knights of
Labor had been dismissed, perhaps for union activity. In New

York employees of an elevated railway struck for shorter hours and better pay. Carnegie appears to take sides with the workers in both, but notes that in each the workers had lost much of their public support by resorting to violence. As usual for that day, he blames this on "a handful of foreign anarchists" (131–34, 142).

In summing up the situation, Carnegie makes a statement which has been widely quoted, pro and con:

> While public sentiment has rightly and unmistakably condemned violence, even in the form for which there is the most excuse, I would have the public give due consideration to the terrible temptation to which the working-man on strike is sometimes subjected. To expect that one dependent on his daily wage for the necessities of life will stand by and see a new man employed in his stead, is to expect much. . . . In all but a very few departments of labor it is unnecessary, and, I think, improper, to subject men to such an ordeal. . . . The employer of labor will find it much more to his interest, wherever possible, to allow his works to remain idle and await the result of a dispute. (144)

Seven years later, following the bloody Homestead strike at his own mill, Carnegie was accused of inconsistency. Hardhearted he was, but not inconsistent. The paragraph sounds very sweet and gentle. But many have overlooked another observation in the same article: "*First.* The "dead line" has been definitely fixed between the forces of disorder and anarchy and those of order. Bomb-throwing means swift death to the thrower. Rioters assembling in numbers and marching to pillage will be remorselessly shot down" (143). As usual, Carnegie was ambivalent. He had sympathy for the suffering worker, but when the decision had to be made between the striker and the steelman's property, he was capitalist first, humanitarian afterward.

A note under the table of contents states that: "The various articles in this volume are reprinted by permission of the publishers of the periodicals in which they originally appeared," and lists these as *Youth's Companion, Century Magazine, North American Review, Forum, Contemporary Review, Fortnightly Review, Nineteenth Century,* and *Scottish Leader.* There is nothing from *Fortnightly Review* included, however, nor would

Carnegie's only contribution to that periodical have been appropriate. The error seems to represent one more instance of Carnegie's inexact memory, and perhaps wishful thinking, for *Fortnightly Review* was a most prestigious journal.

The book attracted even more attention on both sides of the Atlantic than had the original article, and generally drew more favorable reviews, probably because Carnegie was now far more widely known and influential than he had been eleven years previously. As the *Outlook* stated in a two-page review, "Inasmuch as the Author's income far exceeds that of the King of England, and his private fortune exceeds that of the whole people in many principalities, it is doubtful if any moralist since Marcus Aurelius has wielded greater material power; and the fact that in this case the preacher talks, not of the duties which he would lay upon others, but of those which he lays upon himself, lends to his preaching a unique interest."[18]

Commercially the book was a success, being reprinted many times in America and abroad. In 1901 Carnegie added to the volume one more essay, "British Pessimism," which had appeared in *Nineteenth Century and After* in June of that year.[19] It discusses and analyzes the severe depression in Britain at the turn of the century, rightly attributing much of the difficulty to high taxes, imperialism, and the large military and naval budget.

IV   *The Later "Gospel"*

After writing the earlier articles and subsequent to their publication in book form, Carnegie had carried out his long-planned intention of retiring from business, not with his original goal of $50,000 a year in income, but with hundreds of millions in gold bonds worth more than par. Following a brief period of depression in which he bitterly regretted retirement,[20] he had flung himself again into action, writing, speaking and working out ways to give away the fortune he had made.

Seventeen years after the magazine publication of "Wealth," and six after the appearance of the book, Carnegie contributed another article in the series, again to the *North American Review*. At his request, the first essay, with its later designation, had been republished in the September 21, 1906, issue, and on December 7, the final word appeared as "The Gospel of Wealth—II."[21] No reference was made to the original second part, "The Best Fields for Philanthropy."

The article's first words reveal Carnegie's concern with the old subject, and his recognition that legislation, not evolution, would be required, both for breaking up large fortunes, and for securing better distribution: "The problem of wealth will not down. It is obviously so unequally distributed that the attention of civilized man must be attracted to it from time to time. He will ultimately enact the laws needed to produce a more equal distribution."

The article next quotes President Theodore Roosevelt's speech of April 14, 1906, urging graduated gift and inheritance taxes as a necessity to break up large concentrations of wealth. It further cites Carnegie's 1889 article. "See," Carnegie seems to be saying, "I've been telling you this, all the time." And so he had. But with age his devotion to capitalism, if not to capital, had grown stronger. He gives several pages to examples of how fortunes can be made, to show that taking part of the money is just. In every case, he decides, it is community and population growth which have really produced the wealth. He vigorously opposes, as he had before, any income tax. And now he would even except the estate of the man who made the fortune. It is only at the death of his children that the law should operate. (Carnegie now knew he might leave a widow and a daughter, but had no certainty of grandchildren.) Fortunes could be and often were unfairly made; but Britain had passed the point where they could be easily won, and so would America. For the rest, democracy would be trusted to meet such situations as might arise.

V   The Empire of Business

In April 1902—perhaps heartened by the success of his earlier book—Carnegie brought out another collection of his works as *The Empire of Business*. It contains ten of his previously published articles and seven speeches dating from 1885 to 1902. The articles had appeared in the *North American Review*, the

Forum, the *New York Evening Post*, the *New York Tribune*, *Iron Age*, the *New York Journal*, *Youth's Companion*, *Contemporary Review*, *Nineteenth Century*, and *Macmillan's Magazine*, and deal principally with industrial and economic themes.

The most interesting and persuasive one, "The A B C of Money," had been printed in the *North American Review* in 1891, during the "free silver" agitation. It is direct and easily understandable, presenting the argument for a gold standard in the best tradition of the period.

In his "Interests of Labour and Capital," Carnegie stresses education in labor, saying, "In these days of transition and of struggles between labour and capital, to no better purpose can you devote a few of your spare hours than to the study of economic questions."[22] Carnegie practiced what he preached, for he seldom missed an opportunity to learn from leading financiers, bankers, and stockholders about business conditions, and was even able to predict price levels six months in the future without a second thought. But he never explained how a man working eighty-four hours a week at fourteen cents an hour could find "spare hours" or materials for such study.

Although Carnegie stated in "How to Win Fortune" that "The enormous concern of the future is to divide its profits, not among hundreds of idle capitalists who contribute nothing to its success, but among hundreds of its ablest employees, upon whose abilities and exertions success greatly depends,"[23] he nevertheless believed that the best way to bind a man to his work was not to pay him a high salary but give him a share in the business. Carnegie was a pioneer in this policy.

Like its predecessor, *The Empire of Business* proved popular. First issued by Doubleday in 1902, it was taken over by Harper & Brothers the following year, and brought out in simultaneous British and American editions. In a later edition Carnegie added one more chapter, "Does America Hate England?" from the November, 1897, issue of *Contemporary Review*.

VI   Problems of Today

Except for a few later portions of the *Autobiography*, the last book Carnegie wrote was *Problems of Today*. It appeared in

November 1908, and has been largely neglected, even by his biographers. The only one who mentions it is Hendrick,[24] who dismisses it with the statement that it is a collection of "essays, touched up for republication, that had appeared in *Nineteenth Century, Contemporary Review*, the *Century Magazine*, and the like."

Examination discloses that only the first two of its ten chapters include or quote appreciable amounts of his previous material, the final one being a reprint *in toto* of "My Experience with Railway Rates and Rebates" (twenty-two pages), which had appeared in *Century* in March of the year of the book's publication. The first chapter, "Wealth," forty-six pages in length, includes thirteen and a half pages quoted from the 1889 *North American Review* article of the same title, which had formed the basis for *The Gospel of Wealth*. The next, "Labor," includes four pages quoted from "An Employer's View of the Labor Question," published in the *Forum* in April 1886, and another two and a half quoted from that article and a follow-up, "Results of the Labor Struggle," in the same magazine the following August. Elsewhere one and one-half pages are quoted from an address at the opening of the library Carnegie had given to Homestead, Pa., in 1898. Thus a total of forty-five pages of the volume's 207 were taken from his earlier writings, or just over one-fifth.

Additional chapters of the work are concerned with "Wages," "Thrift," "The Land," "Individualism versus Socialism," "Family Relations," and "The Long March Upward." Although little of it is copied or reprinted, it does not contain much that is new, even to Carnegie's thinking. The old themes are there—the advantages of poverty, necessity of thrift, importance of accumulations of capital, and evolutionary social development—the Spencerian march onward and upward.

Carnegie, as age advanced, had obviously become more and more afraid of Socialism, not because of what it might do to him, but its possible effect on the Capitalist system he had helped to shape, and which he loved. Over and over again he argues against endangering the basis of civilization (to him, property) by changing to some new, unproved, and possibly destructive way of meeting social problems. His guides are still Adam Smith, Mill, and Spencer. Changes in the tried and true system would wreck everything—even the family, which would necessarily wind up in Karl Pearson's "complete freedom in the sex-relationship, left to the judgment and taste of . . . men and women."[25] Against this Carnegie sets up his well-loved theme from Goethe: "In the happiest and holiest homes of today, it is not the man who leads the wife upward, but the infinitely purer and more angelic wife whom the husband reverently follows upon the heavenly path."[26] He no longer cries out that "The problem of Wealth will not down," although he recognizes that "our Socialistic friends . . . mean well. . . . No class is moved by worthier impulses." But the danger of Socialist change is that of revolution, as opposed to evolution: "By the nature of its being, the one rule which the human race never can persistently violate is that which proclaims, 'Hold fast to that which has proved itself good.' . . . We believe that the surest and best way . . . is by continued evolution, as in the past, instead of by revolutionary Socialism, which spends its time preaching such changes as are not within measurable distance of attainment, even if they were desirable in themselves."[27]

VII *Summary*

Carnegie had long wrestled with the problem of unequal distribution of wealth. As a youth he was at least a lukewarm Socialist, and by 1868 was seeking to find a compromise with his conscience over practicing what he still called the "worship of the golden calf." Almost twenty years later he felt he had found an answer: the rich man should give away his surplus and inheritance taxes should prevent the family of the unwilling rich man from "burdening" his family with wealth. But no longer was the maker of wealth to give everything away beyond what he needed. Holding a large fortune was proper as long as he gave it away before his death.

By the late 1880s Carnegie had come to recognize the high cost large industry brought in the complete separation and even loss of touch between employer and employees, rich and poor. The condition was actually good, however, because it brought "progress." What later came to be known as the

"American Dream"—that any capable youth could have a Horatio Alger career and become rich—compensated for the want and suffering of others.

Following the severe labor troubles which began in 1887, and even more after bloody Homestead, Carnegie came to feel that the lives of workmen were relatively unimportant, compared with the progress of civilization, which he equated with property. Trusts, cut-throat competition were all right—everything would work out satisfactorily. At last, under the influence of Theodore Roosevelt, he came to recognize that there must be legislation to control abuses. Once again he felt that socialism had a good idea, but it would be dangerous to try it, because it was an untried and uncertain path. It was attempting to do at once what could only be accomplished by a long period of evolution. The one certain wisdom was for mankind to continue doing what had been proved so successful, the amassing of property by the capable, who would then know best what should be done with it.

CHAPTER 7

Proliferous Speaker: 1877-1912

CARNEGIE was one of the most popular and sought-after speakers of his day. Frequently he was called upon to address organizations, and not always those which were interested in acquiring donations. Early in his life, he had formed good speaking habits which helped him in his orations. One ground of Carnegie's freshness of spirit and vehement style, which gained momentum at just the right places, can be found in his own thinking:

> I remember in one of my sweet strolls "ayont the wood mill braes" with a great man, my Uncle Bailie Morrison. . . . I asked him what he thought the most thrilling thing in life. He mused awhile, as was the Bailie's wont, and I said, "I think I can tell you, Uncle." "What is it then, Andrea?" . . . "Well, Uncle, I think that when, in making a speech, one feels himself lifted, as it were, by some divine power into regions beyond himself, in which he seems to soar without effort, and swept by enthusiasm into the expression of some burning truth, which has laid brooding in his soul, throwing policy and prudence to the winds, he feels words whose eloquence surprises himself, burning hot, hissing through him like molten lava coursing the veins, he throws it forth, and panting for breath hears the quick, sharp, explosive roar of his fellow-men in thunder of assent, the precious moment which tells him that the audience is his own, but one soul in it and that his; I think this the supreme moment of life."

To which his uncle responds, "Go! Andrea, ye've hit it!"[1]

Carnegie not only felt this way about speaking, but demonstrated it as well. On the public platform he was a dramatic showman. "Frequently rising to his tiptoes and pumping his short arms vigorously, to his critics in the audience he looked like a bantam rooster ready to crow."[2]

Almost from boyhood he practiced oratory. Carnegie and five

100

of his companions formed a debating society which met in a cobbler shop. Later this same circle of friends became members of the foremost club in the city, about which he wrote in his *Autobiography*:

> Another step which exercised a decided influence over me was joining the "Webster Literary Society."
> I know of no better mode of benefiting a youth than joining such a club as this. Much of my reading became such as had a bearing on forthcoming debates and that gave clearness and fixity to my ideas. The self-possession I afterwards came to have before an audience may very safely be attributed to the experience of the "Webster Society." My two rules for speaking then (and now) were: Make yourself perfectly at home before your audience, and simply talk *to* them, not *at* them. Do not try to be somebody else; be your own self and *talk*, never "orate" until you can't help it.[3]

Among the many goals that he set for himself in 1868 Carnegie listed "pay especial attention to speaking in public."[4] In so doing he discovered a Professor Churchill from Boston, who instructed him in the art of platform oratory.[5]

His convictions concerning oratory were strengthened at the time the Freedom of Dunfermline was conferred upon him in 1877. Carnegie had spoken to his Uncle Bailie Morrison concerning his speech of acceptance, confiding that he desired to say what was in his heart. To which his uncle, an orator himself, replied, "Just say that, Andra [*sic*]; nothing like saying just what you really feel." Carnegie later wrote—

> It was a lesson in public speaking which I took to heart. There is one rule I might suggest for youthful orators. When you stand up before an audience reflect that there are before you only men and women. You should speak to them as you speak to other men and women in daily intercourse. If you are not trying to be something different from yourself, there is no more occasion for embarrassment than if you were talking in your office to a party of your own people—none whatever. . . . Be your own natural self and go ahead. I once asked Colonel Ingersoll, the most effective public speaker I ever heard, to what he attributed his power, "Avoid elocutionists like snakes," he said, "and be yourself."[6]

Another factor which helped to make Carnegie an articulate speaker was hearing the *Messiah* while on the great coaching trip in 1881. He was impressed by the fact that choral groups in England were more careful with their words than choruses in America: "In public as well as in private singing the purity of pronunciation struck us as remarkable. If I ever set up for a music teacher I shall bequeath to my favorite pupil as the secret of success but one word, '*pronunciation.*' "[7]

Carnegie always paid particular attention to the audience when he or others were speaking. During Matthew Arnold's lecture tour of the United States in 1883, Carnegie suggested that the visitor obtain instruction in public speaking from one of the best elocutionists in America at that time—the same Professor Churchill under whom he had studied. His remark came after an unsuccessful speech in which the front row of the audience could barely hear Arnold. Perhaps one of Andrew's best teachers was his mother. When Arnold asked Margaret Carnegie for her opinion in regard to how his oration went, her reply was, "Too meenisterial, Mr. Arnold, too meenisterial."[8]

Carnegie was an adept humorist as well as convincing speaker. As a result, his talks were frequently interrupted by applause, cheering, and laughter. Throughout his addresses, one can detect this buoyant spirit, sense the fervor of his style, and at times almost imagine the enthusiastic response that must have accompanied his orations.

Many of the addresses are available for study. Burton J. Hendrick prints sixteen of them in his collection of Carnegie works as *Miscellaneous Writings.*[9] Carnegie used one in *The Gospel of Wealth*, and seven in *The Empire of Business.*[10] In addition, at least seventy-five were distributed in pamphlet form, some by the thousands. Scores were quoted at length in contemporary newspapers.

I   *Light Speeches*

Self-trained to think on his feet, Carnegie was a master of impromptu speaking and repartee. Perhaps the best example of his off-the-cuff manner still preserved is the one entitled "Industrial Pennsylvania," which was given in 1900 before the

Pennsylvania Society of New York.[11] To his surprise two earlier speakers talked on much the same subject. In his introduction Carnegie said, "I find myself most peculiarly situated here to-night. The gentleman on my left, the Assistant Attorney-General, expresses his anxiety to take my pocket book and the gentleman on my right has stolen my speech. I have given much thought to the matter but I think that I have hit upon the right plan at last for successfully disposing of my surplus wealth—I must call in the members of his profession, who are willing to talk on all sides of a question and who stand ready to take money from either or all sides."

Then he continued, "Gentlemen, I am here in a double capacity to-night, as my invitation was first as President of St. Andrew's Society, and the second as a devoted Pennsylvanian. . . . I cannot speak to you to-night of 'Industrial Pennsylvania,' because it has been spoken of twice already, and, as Governor [James A.] Beaver says, 'Pennsylvania, like Massachusetts, needs no encomium.' There she stands. She speaks for herself." (Here Carnegie was continuing the paraphrase on Daniel Webster's famous speech on secession.) Reflecting his Scottish pride, Carnegie said, "I am gratified at the evidence given here to-night of the wish of everybody who has spoken, wherever born, or however born, to be born again, that he might have at least the right to claim some Scotch blood in his veins."

Finally Carnegie proceeded to speak on his assigned subject, emphasizing the importance of home commerce. In rationalizing Pennsylvania's population decrease in the 1880 census compared to the increase in New York, he commented tongue-in-cheek, "Now it will be said by the New Yorker that [Pennsylvanians] come here for commercial reasons. Don't, gentlemen New Yorkers, entertain for a moment that mistaken idea. It is the missionary spirit which prompts them to go over to you and which is stirring the world today."

Carnegie shifted to lofty tones for his conclusion: "Pennsylvania products . . . shall continue to be the guiding star to teach all people the true path to a higher civilization and continue to give the foremost place among the states of the Union to the Keystone State, the birthplace of the nation."

"The Scotch-American," Carnegie's speech delivered at the

annual dinner of the St. Andrew's Society in New York, is another example of his light manner of speaking.[12] He launched into his subject with, "This is, indeed, the age of instantaneous photography. I appear before you to-night commissioned to kodak, develop and finish the Scotsman at home, in four minutes; in four minutes more to picture him in America, and in two minutes more to celebrate the union of the two varieties, and place before you the ideal character of the world, the best flower in the garden, the first-prize chrysanthemum—the Scotch-American."

A later statement of grandiose exultation produced much laughter: "It is only through their union that the crowning mercy has been bestowed upon the world, and perfection at last attained in the new variety known as the Scotch-American, who in himself combines, in one perfect whole, the best qualities and all the virtues of both, and stands before the world shining for all, the sole possessor of these united talents, traits, characteristics and virtues, rare in their several excellencies and wonderful in their combination." Continuing in the same vein, Carnegie expressed his true opinion, that racial admixture made for the improvement of society. In ridiculing European aristocracy he said, "The result of lack of fusion between the races is seen in the royal families of Europe, most of them are diseased, many weak-minded, not a few imbecile, and none of them good for much." Another statement brought more laughter and applause: "Scotch wives for American husbands is a fusion which I am told is hard to beat, and I have a very decided opinion, which many of you have good reason, I know, to endorse, that Scotch husbands for American wives is an alliance which cannot be equalled."

Reflecting his belief in the importance of meager beginnings, Carnegie described Scotland as having the "bracing influence of poverty, uncursed by the evils of luxury." His Scottish blood statement, "the land of Wallace, Knox, Scott and Burns belongs not to itself alone, but to the world," was again met with applause.

At times Carnegie made comments even when it was not his turn to speak. During an occasion at which he was to present a light address, the speaker before him said, "If I am a victim to be thrown to the lions, as our toastmaster has said, my fears are the less because men who are thrown to the lions are the ones who in the nature of the case cannot make an after-dinner speech." At this Carnegie called out clearly, "The Prophet Daniel did."[13]

II *Peace Speeches*

For many years one of Carnegie's first principles had been peace—a total prevention of war. Naturally this became a theme of many of his addresses. His hostility to war stemmed from early youth, when he attended peace demonstrations in Dunfermline. Between the years 1901 and 1910, he was involved in very many such projects, and it is not surprising that he chose the subject "A League of Peace" for his second Rectorial Address to the students of St. Andrews.[14]

He began by presenting noble ideals, encouraging the students to "leave the world a little better than you found it." He then cited some social evils which had disappeared—polygamy, slavery, and dueling—but stressed that the most hated one still remained. Commencing with a quotation from Rousseau, who said, "War is the foulest fiend ever vomited forth from the mouth of Hell," he continued to recite the words of nearly seventy other important men who held similar opinions, ending with General Sherman's "War is Hell."

Concluding with a passage from Scripture—"When men shall beat their swords into ploughshares"—he stressed the need for a League of Peace. Carnegie appealed to the students, male and female alike, to move "onward and upward," putting all else aside in their concentration on a means to end all wars—preventing them before they happen.

Five years later, on March 10, 1910, Carnegie in his speech " 'Honor' and International Arbitration" again lashed out against war.[15] Addressing the Peace Society at Guildhall in London, he began with a lament upon the recent death of King Edward, and expressed the hope that Edward's successor would continue with efforts of peace. Later in his oration he elaborated more in detail on the former sovereign.

He spoke of the changes in war, tactics not being as savage

as they formerly had been, saying that the real problem was not war itself but the ever-present threat and danger of war, its continuous preparation, and the distrust of one nation for another. Asserting that partial disarmament is not enough, he advocated peaceful arbitration as a solution. Since before the turn of the century he had stressed in many speeches and magazine articles his conviction that civilized man must substitute arbitration for war. He praised Taft for his support of arbitration: "Let all friends of peace hail President Taft as our leader." (But at a later date, when the U.S. Senate rejected the arbitration treaty, he was quick to blame the president.)[16]

Disputing the belief that "war is the nursery of heroes," Carnegie mentioned industrial heroes and his Hero Fund. He again quoted Sherman as he had in his peace speech to the St. Andrew's students, ending with his pet Spencerian notion that man moves "ever upward and onward toward perfection."

III *Gift Speeches*

As a result of his many benefactions, Carnegie was called upon to speak at numerous dedications. Two early speeches are found in *Our Coaching Trip*. In his address at Dunfermline on the occasion of the laying of the memorial stone for his gift of a free library in 1881, Carnegie greeted his audience as "workingmen and women of Dunfermline." He was proud to claim the title of workingman himself, and "one who like yourselves has toiled with my hands . . . you have Shakespeare, the mightiest of all intellects and you have your own genius, Burns, the ploughman." He continued, "It is impossible that any act which I may perform in after life can give me the gratification flowing from this as you, by your free and generous use of the library, enable me to indulge the sweet thought that it has been my privilege to bestow upon Dunfermline, my native town, A Free Library, which has proved itself a foundation of good to my fellow-townsmen."[17]

When he was asked to speak following the swimming competition at the baths he had donated to the town, Carnegie said, "Great Britain will continue to rule the waves about as long as I should like to prophesy any nation would rule anything;

and I think that it is incumbent for that reason that the sons of Great Britain should learn to be at home in the waves which we expect them to continue to rule. However, there is no longer any question about this, that Dunfermline has begun to see the advantage, and she will no doubt soon recognize the duty of teaching all her sons to feel this confidence at least, that they were not born to be drowned."[18]

In 1891 Carnegie spoke on the occasion of the laying of the foundation stone for the Peterhead Free Library in Scotland.[19] He stressed how other nations had followed different paths, "Some built upon military or artistic attainments, but Scotland upon the general education of her people." Using a familiar nautical theme, he said, "There is no helm that steers so true in the voyage of life as Common Sense." Later he expounded upon the influence of the sea: "To be in daily contact with the sea—nay! more weird still, nightly contact; to brave its tempests; to draw from its bosom the means of subsistence, must necessarily strengthen what is bold and adventurous in man." And, as always in referring to education, he quoted Knox: "I will never rest until there is a school in every parish in Scotland."

Disliking the dead languages all his life, Carnegie emphasized the importance of the "all-round intelligent man," as opposed to "men from college who knew so much of the skirmishes of the tribes of Greece and Rome ... but as we say in America, 'didn't know beans.'"

He spoke of the importance of a free library, especially for working men, and stressed good labor relations, saying, "Every Free Library in these days should contain upon its shelves all contributions bearing upon the relations of labour and capital. . . ." He also emphasized the importance of a good librarian and of circulating libraries. Pointing out his belief in distributing surplus wealth, he suggested that a good way for small amounts of money to be put to the best use was through donations of books to libraries.

The Scottish blood theme came through when he spoke of immigration: "There is no land upon the earth which would not only waive all examination, but receive with open arms him who is privileged to say in response to all inquiries, 'I am a Scotchman.' The only objection might be [quoting Abram

S. Hewitt of New York], 'We are always somewhat afraid when we get a Scotchman that ere long he may own the works.'"

Scottish prejudice is reflected in his words: "The proud position occupied by our race comes, no doubt, partly from the bracing climate of the north, and from the generations of no less bracing oppression which our mountain home has had to encounter in its resolute and successful struggle for the preservation of its nationality; but, without doubt, it flows chiefly from the fact that Scotchmen have been better and more thoroughly educated for generations than other races." The words are reminiscent of a statement in his *Autobiography*: "The intensity of a Scottish boy's patriotism . . . constitutes a real force in his life to the very end. If the source of my stock of that prime article—courage—were studied, I am sure the final analysis would find it founded upon Wallace, the hero of Scotland. . . . The true Scotsman will not find reason in after years to lower the estimate he has formed of his own country."[20]

In 1903 Carnegie paid tribute to eight different towns within a week's time, and other gift speeches were made on the same tour. When laying the foundation stone for the free library of Dingwall, Carnegie said, "This stone is level, this stone is plumb, this stone is truly laid and may the blessing of God rest upon the work of this day and upon this library when it is completed." Adapting from Gamaliel's speech in Acts 5, he added, "If this thing be of men, it will fail, but if it be of God it must stand."[21]

At Tain for the dedication of the town hall, Carnegie reflected his Scottish prejudice in a humorous vein: "In one case I heard of, a man's claim [to Scottish blood] was based upon the fact that his grandmother had a Scotch nurse." Later in his speech he advised the young people to become interested in music and drama, taking advantage of the chance to perform in the new hall.[22]

When laying the memorial stone of the public school in Kilmarnock, Carnegie repeated the hope of John Knox for a school in every parish in Scotland. At times Carnegie wandered from his prepared text, and openly admitted it. As always, he brought up his hatred for war, saying, "That is not in my notes. But I like to make digressions when the spirit moves me." About education he said, "It has been said you can educate a man too much. You might as well tell me you could have a man too sober."[23]

At the dedication of the free library in Govan, Carnegie quoted twice the maxim "We only hate those we do not know," and prophesied that wars shall cease when nations get to know one another. Reflecting other favorite themes, he said that the "best worship of God, is serving man," and "the finest heritage for a young man is poverty."[24]

In laying the foundation stone of the free library in Waterford, Ireland, Carnegie stated that this was his first speech in that country, although he admitted, "It is not my first speech before an Irish audience, for I have had often to speak in the city of New York, and you all know what an Irish city that is. And I have spoken in Pittsburgh, and you know it is of a Scotch-Irish character." And in words of flattery he said, "All the world likes Ireland."[25]

At Limerick for the laying of the library foundation stone, Carnegie commented on how much the Irish and Scotch had in common, and went on to say, "The community that is not willing to maintain a library is not worthy of having one." He also emphasized that free libraries are especially for the toiling masses. The rich can buy books of their own. And again he stressed the importance of a good librarian versus a poor one.[26]

During the laying of the memorial stone for the library at Cork, he predicted that if the English-speaking race would reunite, they could decree peace and enforce it—again the same familar theme, peace, or, if necessary, war for peace.[27]

An important speech on this tour was addressed to the Iron and Steel Institute at Barrow, and again included the ideal of English-speaking nations enforcing peace among all nations, with Carnegie's regret that an ocean instead of a prairie separated Europe from the New World.[28]

The continuous enthusiasm of his audiences and the sense of achievement certainly must have inspired Carnegie in his dispersal of surplus wealth. To his speech at the laying of a cornerstone at Ayr, the audience responded by giving him a standing ovation, waving hats and handkerchiefs and making loud cheers before he even uttered a word.[29] Throughout the address, Carnegie gave voice to his Scottish patriotism, saying,

"All nations and all peoples love Scotland." Quoting from Robert Burns, he reflected his dream of peace and brotherhood, "When man to man the world o'er, shall brithers be an' a' that."

Even during his marriage tour of Scotland in 1887, Carnegie was requested to speak on numerous occasions. Within three days he assisted in the ceremony of unveiling the busts of Walter Scott, John Knox, and George Buchanan in the Wallace Monument at Stirling; lectured in Glasgow on "Home Rule in America"; and christened a Mexican steamer and inaugurated a public library in Grangemouth, all with the assistance of Mrs. Carnegie. Reflecting deep-rooted patriotism in his speeches during this tour, he emphasized especially the brotherhood of man and the union of English-speaking nations. In his "Home Rule" speech, he quoted Tennyson:

And where is the hope of that great day which the poet sings of—when the drum shall beat no longer, when the battleflags are furled,
In the Parliament of Man, the Federation of the World?[30]

IV Speeches to Students

Carnegie on many occasions was requested to speak before student bodies. One of his favorite themes and methods of approach in talking to his young listeners was the figure of embarking upon the sea of life. He made frequent use of nautical terms and expressions such as "set sail with clear papers," "propitious gales," "wretched brothers drifting past," "brave mariners," "storm-beaten," and "my young untried sailors."

Carnegie's address to the graduating class of medical students at Bellevue Hospital in New York in 1885 is an example of this nautical theme.[31] In the beginning he said:

No voyager ever sailed from end to end upon summer seas in undisturbed calm. Always there come
        The visitation of the winds,
            Who take the ruffian billows by the top,
        Curling their monstrous heads.

These angry gusts call for the boldest, steadiest seamanship, a level head, a strong arm, and a heart that is not afraid.

And closing with the same theme:

Most anxious to say to you in parting the words which may prove most beneficial upon your voyage on life's troubled seas, I leave you with this expression of my deliberate opinion, which I ask you to write upon your hearts, making it at once your talisman and compass to direct your course: By maintaining intact the noble traditions of your profession, and handing these down untarnished to your successors, you can best dignify your own lives and best perform the highest service of which you are capable to humanity.

In talking to the young men at the Curry Commercial College on June 23, 1885, Carnegie told how he started his career sweeping the office: he concluded by congratulating the students upon being hard-working poor men who started at the bottom, for "He is the probable dark horse that you had better watch."[32] During this speech Carnegie encouraged the students to aim high and "be king in your dreams," just as he later would with the Cornell students in his address in 1907.[33] From experience, he pointed out several conditions essential for success—honesty, truthfulness and fair-dealing, along with avoiding liquor, speculation, and endorsement of other men's notes. And again using his pet maxim, "Put all your eggs in one basket, and then watch the basket."[34]

Likewise, Carnegie, in his lecture delivered at Union College in Schenectady, N.Y., in January 1895, emphasized, "Thou shalt earn thy bread by the sweat of thy brow," and "The richest heritage a young man can be born to is poverty."[35]

To the students of Cornell University on January 11, 1896, Carnegie again stressed that theme: the poor boy has usually one strong guarantee of future industry and ambitious usefulness—he is not burdened with wealth; it is necessary that he make his own way in the world.[36]

Gradually, as Carnegie gained confidence and realized he had become an international figure, his college speeches became less the advice of a successful man to beginners and more often pronouncements of his beliefs on world affairs, as with the rectorial address cited above.

Perhaps Carnegie's most outspoken speech for students was one on religion, intended for students at St. Andrew's University at his installation as Lord Rector in 1902. But although this address would be appropriate today, it was not acceptable then. Carnegie was ahead of his time. Due to the impact that such a speech as he had prepared would have upon the students, Carnegie was asked to write another one using a subject other than religion. As a result, he delivered one on "The Industrial Ascendancy of the World" instead.[37] Using his familiar nautical theme, Carnegie began, "My annual voyages across the Atlantic rarely yield much time for reading. I am so fond of the deck and the bridge that my time is usually spent there, reveling in the tumbling sea; the higher the waves the greater being the exhilaration."[38]

He then elaborated upon economic and business changes in the world, and the growth of nations in wealth and population, the social condition and aptitudes of their people, natural resources, prospects, ambitions, and national policy. Summing up the laws bearing upon the material position of nations, he went on to compare Europe's position with America's. As in so many other speeches, he stressed international peace, and in so doing praised the Emperor of Russia, citing the Hague Conference which established a permanent tribunal composed of able men from various nations. He also mentioned the German Emperor, who had stimulated industrial action. As a result of this speech, Wilhelm II, after reading his address, invited Carnegie to visit him for discussion upon the subject. This led to further meetings, with other influential statesmen becoming aware of Carnegie's doctrine that American-European competition is not a case of nation against nation, but instead continent against continent.[39]

The original speech he had intended for the St. Andrew's students was published at last in 1933 among Carnegie's miscellaneous writings. His confession of religious faith is personally very revealing. From this address one can readily understand the influences which helped determine his lifelong beliefs and convictions. This relatively unknown speech reveals his depth of religion and personality more than any other he wrote, and therefore should be given fuller attention.

The original speech included the nautical theme, referring to students as the "untried sailor cadets who are about to launch upon the voyage of life."[40] More importantly, in relating his own experiences to the students, he wrote—

The clear line drawn here between theology and religion, the one changing and the other surviving, the one of man and the other in man, I trust you will always keep in mind in your ministry as teachers of men.

When my young brain began to think, these were one and inseparable. I knew no difference between them. The Shorter Catechism, Confession of Faith, and all the structure of theology, the work of men of an ignorant past, were part of the one divine revelation. Theology was religion and religion was theology.... Today they are distinct as the stiff, dead frame is from the living picture.... So far have we advanced in one generation. (295)

He mentioned how he had been influenced as a working boy by the books made available to him in Colonel Anderson's library and how at this time in his life, "all at sea" with "No creed, no system ... all was chaos," he had discovered Herbert Spencer and Charles Darwin and at last was able to say, " 'That settles the question!' I had found at last the guides which led me to the temple of man's real knowledge upon earth.... I was upon firm ground, and with every year of my life since there has come less dogmatism, less theology, but greater reverence" (297).

Later he discredited miracles, quoting Matthew Arnold, who wrote, "The case against miracles is closed. They do not happen," and Thomas Fuller, who said, "Miracles are the swaddling clothes of the infant church" (298, 305).

Mentioning how his travels had influenced him, Carnegie told how he had witnessed all the religions of the world, and whether in the name of "God, Jah, Jehovah, Jove, Brahm, Baal, Buddha," among others, "all the earth worships the true God.... The unknown had left no nation without religion" (309–11). Ever predicting and confident of the future, Carnegie added,

"New and mighty truths are yet to be revealed at intervals, and we are to see present truths more perfectly, probably to the end of time" (318).

Finally, stressing the tasks of "improving our fellow-men" and "obeying the judge within," and noting "that the worship most acceptable to God is service to man," he ended with a favorite saying, "science ... has revealed ... the divine law of his being which leads man ever steadily upward" (319).

V *Speeches on the Black Problem*

For a person who felt that race was of ultimate importance in explaining the progress of Anglo-Saxon peoples, Carnegie's ideas in regard to the Negro were surprisingly flexible. Although his views on black rights and achievements would be considered lukewarm by today's standards, he was nonetheless well ahead of his time in this respect. There were few Americans in that period who even considered equal rights for this minority tolerable, much less desirable.

Carnegie had never come into close contact with any blacks except for a few outstanding leaders, and had almost no knowledge of their condition in the South or even in the ghettos of the North. But he had come to have a certain respect for the yellow and brown during his trip around the world, and this may have affected his outlook on the subject. There was a popular upsurge of interest in Southern education during the first decade of the twentieth century, and his involvement in the field manifested itself alike in words and benefactions.

Speaking as chairman of a joint educational conference on this subject in New York on February 12, 1904, Carnegie began by pointing out that Lincoln did his part in freeing the slaves; but since "he only is a freeman whom education makes free ... it remains for us, the followers of that leader of men, to continue and complete it." He upheld the right of blacks in the North to vote, since they were in a minority. But in the South, where ignorant whites and Negroes made up a majority, he urged that there continue to be an educational requirement for suffrage.[41]

Again, when asked to speak in October 1907 before the

Philosophical Institution of Edinburgh, Carnegie chose as his theme "The Negro in America."[42] In this address he took up where his earlier one had left off. He cited the early history of the race in America, and assessed very aptly—for that day— the principal factors which led up to a break between North and South on the subject of slavery, the enfranchisement of blacks, and the consequent bitterness among their former masters. Now, "after a period of fifty [*sic*] years, we are tonight to inquire whether the American Negro has proved his capacity to develop and improve." Carnegie proposed three tests. Has the black proved himself able to live in contact with civilization, and increase as a freeman, or does he slowly die out like the American Indian, Maori, or Hawaiian? Could and would he seek education and achieve it? Could and would he become a man of property? All these he answered in the affirmative, supporting his answer to each with an array of statistics provided for him largely by his close friend and beneficiary, Booker T. Washington, and the faculty of Tuskegee Institute.

Next, he cited the means of improvement, and the careers of many outstanding blacks, then (and some of them until recently) neglected by historians—poets, educators, astronomers, and successful businessmen—and their part in a rapidly expanding South. As Wall has pointed out, it was like a black *Triumphant Democracy*, all "sunshine, sunshine, sunshine," which would hardly be recognizable to the Southern sharecropper or the inhabitant of the Northern black ghetto.[43] Neither was Carnegie—nor did he allow his hearers to depart—oblivious to the fact that "all that has been done, encouraging as it undoubtedly is, yet is trifling compared to what remains to be done.—The bright spots have been brought to your notice, but these are only small points surrounded by great areas of darkness. The sun spreading light over all has not yet arisen, altho there are not wanting convincing proofs that her morning beams begin to gild the mountain tops."

Carnegie did not share the general and long-standing fear of an admixture of races: "What is to be the final result of the black and white races living together in centuries to come need not concern us. They may remain separate and apart as now, or may inter-mingle." He closed by citing the words of

Lyman Abbott: "Never in the history of man has a race made such educational and material progress in forty years as the American Negro."[44]

VI *National Mores*

On numerous occasions Carnegie spoke about social mores. His speech delivered before the Scottish Charitable Society of Boston is a fair example of this.[45]

In this charming essay, Carnegie stated that New England rightfully should be called "New Scotland," for she has more in common with that country than England. In comparing Scotland and New England, Carnegie pointed out the fact that they had a common foe, England. For independence, he said, "the Puritan left his home to establish himself in New England," and his "fellow Presbyterians in Scotland, instead of leaving the old home, remained there and fought the same issue...."

Carnegie's first speech in New York, an impromptu one before the Nineteenth Century Club, on "The Aristocracy of the Dollar," also dealt with the mores of the time.[46] After sitting through three speeches that evening, Carnegie, when given the opportunity, disputed the third speaker, Thomas Wentworth Higginson, on three points. He objected first to Higginson's statement that "the aristocracy of the dollar has inferior manners." Also disputing that the aristocracy of Britain is finer looking than any other class, he said, "Let any visitor see the House of Lords when it is filled.... Upon such an occasion one would really think, as he watches the peers pass, or rather hobble in, that every reformatory, asylum or home for incurables, in Britain, had been asked to send up to Westminster fair specimens of its inmates.... An aristocracy of birth alone has never been able to sustain itself."

He objected next to the assertion that the "aristocracy of the dollar is selfish and dangerous." Carnegie said that the aristocracy of birth is most selfish, "that class which, during life, gives the least proportion of its revenues for the good of others.... As to the danger of the Dollar I must dissent in toto.... Great fortunes ... are built up by life-long devotion to that end; by the exercise of ... prudence, forethought, energy ... and self-denial."

Finally, he objected to the statement that the "aristocracy of the dollar is not self-respecting." He directed the question to Higginson, "whether the reign of the aristocracy of intellect does not exist in American Society to-day, rather than that of the dollar." Carnegie concluded that "in the final aristocracy the question will not be how he was born or what he owns, nor how he has worshipped God, but how has he served Man."

Carnegie spent little time in Pittsburgh after moving to New York, but was still in close touch thirty years later when he accepted an invitation to speak before the Pittsburgh Chamber of Commerce. He opened by complimenting the city on its Chamber: "Your members are men experienced in affairs, and, therefore, upon all business questions. The united chambers of commerce, in older lands, speak upon business questions with great authority—so must they soon with us, and always with increasing authority.... It will not be claimed by the most extreme exponents of democracy that the masses of the people can or do form sound judgments of themselves upon intricate public questions, but ... the masses of our people are so intelligent as to be able to weigh what men of special knowledge lay before them."[47] Pittsburgh had become a "two class" city, and the function of democracy was to teach the masses to follow the leading businessmen and men of wealth.

VII *Summary*

Ever one to grasp any opportunity to express his ideas, Carnegie was never happier than when he appeared before an appreciative and cheering crowd.

In style and general development his addresses vary little from his earliest to his latest period. He used a quick and deft approach to catch the interest and if possible the hearts of his audience; interlarded his arguments with his favorite truisms and maxims; and lightened the heavier parts with humor and witty anecdotes. Yet it is only on the surface that his speeches are the same from his early to his later periods. His rugged individualism continued, and became even stronger than in the days of his youth. But his liberalism gradually extended only toward those in agreement with him or willing to go along with his direction. The man who had believed in no aristocracy except that of ideas gradually approached belief in an aristocracy of power. His faith in democracy was skating on very thin ice when he denied that "the masses" were able to form sound judgments by themselves. When he declared himself "the Laird of Pittencrief" he considered it a joke, but few English landlords could have spoken or acted more paternally or autocratically than he.

CHAPTER 8

The Biographer: 1889-1909

THE personality of Andrew Carnegie, his likes and dislikes, his characteristics and familiar themes are clearly reflected in everything he wrote, but most obviously in his biographical works. These are five—His *Autobiography*; *James Watt*, and three pamphlet speeches: *Ezra Cornell*, *Edwin M. Stanton*, and *William Chambers*. All show the frequent use of truisms and proverbs, intensely personal outlook, flair for the dramatic and quotations from literary classics so pervasive in everything he wrote. And all attribute to the subjects many of the author's tastes, ideas and preferences.

Although his *Autobiography* and other biographic attempts are readable and enjoyable, Carnegie's work is often inexact and prone to error.[1] He continually inserts passages from Shakespeare and the Scottish poets—oftenest Scott and Burns—usually without identifying the sources. Often these are inexactly quoted, either from reliance on memory or to adapt the material to some point he seeks to make. This neglect in researching or checking a subject became more pronounced with advancing age. He would press his convictions on the reader just as he had tried to force democracy on Britain during his newspaper publishing days, sometimes omitting or changing facts in order to support his theories. The persistent nature he evidenced in business can be seen in his writing.

Among the themes that Carnegie uses most often in the biographies are devotion to his mother, Scottish patriotism, hero worship, importance of childhood poverty, significance of trifles, brotherhood, and international peace. Carnegie, with the vision of an idealist, had an irrepressible habit of predicting the future, looking forward as well as backward, and with varying accuracy in either case. A friend wrote: "His views are truly large and prophetic,"[2] but the crystal ball was often clouded.

I *The Autobiography*

The question oftenest asked about any autobiography is whether the book is really necessary. There is no doubt as to the value of the *Autobiography of Andrew Carnegie*. Many encouraged him to write it. As Gilder said: "He is well worth Boswellizing, but I am urging him to be 'his own Boswell.' "[3] John C. Van Dyke, who was chosen to revise the memoirs after Carnegie's death, wrote, "He should be allowed to tell the tale in his own way, and enthusiasm, even extravagance in recitation should be received as a part of the story. The quality of the man may underlie exuberance of spirit, as truth may be found in apparent exaggeration. Therefore, in preparing these chapters for publication the editor has done little more than arrange the material chronologically and sequentially so that the narrative might run on unbrokenly to the end."[4]

Louise Whitfield Carnegie wrote in the Preface: "After retiring from active business my husband yielded to the earnest solicitations of friends, both here and in Great Britain, and began to jot down from time to time recollections of his early days. . . . For a few weeks each summer we retired to our little bungalow on the moors at Aultnagar to enjoy the simple life, and it was there that Mr. Carnegie did most of his writing. . . . He was thus engaged in July, 1914, when the war clouds began to gather. . . . These memoirs ended at that time."[5]

Although these can hardly be considered unbiased views, there is evidence—even aside from the book's wide public acceptance—that Carnegie's contemporaries shared the feeling. Mrs. Carnegie must have known, however, that her husband had actually begun his autobiography in 1889. Hendrick quotes from a Carnegie letter to William E. Gladstone in January 1891:

More than one wise friend has insisted that even I should dictate the story of my career. I promised, and the summer before last, when at Cluny, I spent about an hour every morning—when the conditions were not tempting for fishing or outdoor excursions—in sitting before the fire and gazing into it, recounting to myself, as it were, the incidents of my life. A clever stenographer took down the words, and at intervals transcribed them. The result was that before I knew it I had spoken about six hundred pages, making a book equal to my *Triumphant Democracy* and *Round the World* put together. This manuscript has been laid aside for some future editor—I trust a discreet one—to condense.[6]

The material revised from time to time formed the basis for Carnegie's *Autobiography* in its present form. If Carnegie's figures are accurate here, Van Dyke must have omitted from 40 to almost 50 percent of the manuscript, depending on whether the author refers to the original length of his first travel book, or the expanded form commercially published.

Van Dyke recognized and implied in his Editor's Note, that the *Autobiography* is far from being historically accurate. Relying upon a failing memory, Carnegie forgot things or wrote of events the way he wished they had been. An outstanding instance is his account of the early partnership with T. T. Woodruff in his first sleeping-car venture. In his fine biography of the steel magnate, Wall comments on the highly imaginative account taken from Carnegie's *Triumphant Democracy*: "It is a typical Carnegie story, replete with all the stock situations of popular melodrama: the shy, unworldly inventor, the crude, hand-made model, the chance meeting with the bold young business executive, who in a flashing moment of truth recognizes genius when he sees it. There is even the mysterious green bag, in which the stranger carries his invention. It is all too pat and too familiar, but those commentators upon Carnegie's life who have dealt with this incident have accepted his story in every detail. . . . Woodruff wrote to his alleged discoverer: 'Your arrogance spurred you up to make the statements recorded in your book, which is misleading and so far from the true facts of the case and so damaging to your friend of old as to merit his rebuke. You must have known before you ever saw me that there were many sleeping cars furnished with my patent seats and couches running from a number of railways. . . .' "[7]

The account that Wall and Woodruff refer to was the

following passage in Carnegie's *Triumphant Democracy*: "A tall, spare, farmer-looking kind of man...wished me to look at an invention he had made. With that he drew from a green bag (as it were for lawyers' briefs) a small model of a sleeping berth for railway cars. He had not spoken a minute, before, like a flash, the whole range of discovery burst upon me. 'Yes,' I said, 'that is something which this continent must have.'"[8] Yet despite Woodruff's refutation, Carnegie repeats virtually the same account in his *Autobiography*.[9]

Of all Carnegie's many themes, devotion to his mother is most vivid in *The Autobiography* and overshadows much of his writing. Although he expresses admiration for his father on various occasions, he focuses most of his attention on her, with more than thirty references in the book. Illustrative of this Carnegie writes the following: "Perhaps some day I may be able to tell the world something of this heroine, but I doubt it. I feel her to be sacred to myself and not for others to know. None could ever really know her—I alone did that. After my father's early death she was all my own. The dedication of my first [commercially published] book tells the story. It was 'To my favorite Heroine My Mother'" (6). No doubt his early dependence upon his mother and hers upon him made them become more close than the average Oedipus complex. Again he writes: "Walter Scott said of Burns that he had the most extraordinary eye he ever saw in a human being. I can say as much for my mother" (32).

On a few occasions Carnegie included his father in the exaltation of his mother: "There was nothing that heroine did not do in the struggle we were making for elbow room in the western world. Father's long factory hours tried his strength, but he, too, fought the good fight like a hero, and never failed to encourage me" (37).

Fortunately for Carnegie's wife, he transferred this same adoration to her. He wrote in reference to Louise Whitfield: "It is now twenty years since Mrs. Carnegie entered and changed my life, a few months after the passing of my mother....My life has been made so happy by her that I cannot imagine myself living without her guardianship" (209).

Another familiar theme of Carnegie's *Autobiography* is his

Scottish heritage. The description of his departure as a child from Scotland, upon hearing the old abbey bell ring, makes us realize his keen devotion to his homeland: "Never can there come to my ears on earth, nor enter so deep into my soul, a sound that shall haunt and subdue me with its sweet, gracious, melting power as that did" (26). And upon a return trip to his native land he tells of his mother's and his reaction: "Her heart was so full she could not restrain her tears, and the more I tried to make light of it or to soothe her, the more she was overcome. For myself, I felt as if I could throw myself upon the sacred soil and kiss it" (106).

The theme of patriotism may be observed early in *The Autobiography.* Seldom has there lived a man who was more patriotic than Andrew Carnegie—true-blue Scotsman and star-spangled American through and through. He readily acknowledged: "I can truly say in the words of Burns that there was then and there created in me a vein of Scottish prejudice (or patriotism) which will cease to exist only with life" (15).

Later Carnegie transferred much of this feeling to his adopted land, writing *Triumphant Democracy* to prove its superiority to Britain (318–20). Most assuredly Carnegie would not have taken such a position on first coming to America, for his strong patriotic ties surpassed any that he could have felt for another country at that time. In his own words—

It remains for maturer years and wider knowledge to tell us that every nation has its heroes, its romance, its traditions, and its achievements; and while the true Scotsman will not find reason in after years to lower the estimate he has formed of his own country and of its position even among the larger nations of the earth, he will find ample reason to raise his opinion of other nations because they all have much to be proud of—quite enough to stimulate their sons so to act their parts as not to disgrace the land that gave them birth.

It was years before he could write this, for as Carnegie said, "My heart was in Scotland" (18).

Carnegie always relied strongly on his belief in the purity of Scottish blood. For instance, he notes that upon meeting the German emperor, he had said, "Your Majesty, I now own

King Malcolm's tower in Dunfermline—he from whom you derive your precious heritage of Scottish blood" (355). Along with this intense loyalty, one can perceive Carnegie's persistent hero-worship. In his own words, when he had to face some obstacle he would ask himself, "what Wallace would have done and what a Scotsman ought to do" (34).

But the hero-worship was not confined to his Scottish inheritance. He greatly admired many of his contemporaries as well. Of his early employer and friend he writes, "Mr. [Thomas A.] Scott was one of the most delightful superiors that anybody could have and I soon became warmly attached to him. He was my great man and all the hero worship that is inherent in youth I showered upon him" (67). He also notes that in later years he showed similar devotion for Herbert Spencer and John Morley, among others.

Another popular theme that Carnegie emphasizes intermittently in the *Autobiography* is the importance of meager beginnings. He says of his family's hard times, "This is where the children of honest poverty have the most precious of all advantages of those of wealth." And then two themes in one: "The mother, nurse, cook, governess, teacher, saint, all in one: the father, exemplar, guide, counselor and friend! Thus were my brother and I brought up. What has the child of millionaire or nobleman that counts compared to such a heritage?" (30). In another passage he comments, "Let him look out for the 'dark horse' in the boy who begins by sweeping out the office" (41).

Carnegie lays emphasis on the importance of trifles, especially in regard to business matters. Remarking about a personal experience which was the deciding point in an important bid for his Keystone Bridge Company he writes, "That visit proved how much success turns upon trifles" (118). And again, concerning his merger with George M. Pullman, "One may learn, from an incident which I had from Mr. Pullman himself, by what trifles important matters are sometimes determined" (154). Along the same line he points out the significance of a slight notice of a kind word: "I am indebted to these trifles for some of the happiest attentions and the most pleasing incidents of my life" (82). And then an entire passage on the same subject, ending with, "The young should remember that upon trifles the best gifts of the gods often hang" (35).

It is easy to see the origins of these motifs in Carnegie's early experiences. But we search in vain for the source of his devotion to peace in an era in which almost every other ambitious youngster dreamed of military prowess. Frequently in his *Autobiography*, as well as his other writings and in his actions, he evidenced his concern for international peace and his love of brotherhood. These ideals he acknowledges. "Peace, at last between English-speaking peoples, must have been early in my thoughts" (270). And again he speaks of himself as "saddened and indignant that in the nineteenth century the most civilized race, as we consider ourselves, still finds men willing to adopt as a profession—until lately the only profession for gentlemen—the study of the surest means of killing other men" (323).

A disturbing factor in his life which Carnegie expresses in the latter part of the *Autobiography* is his concern over losing former friends with advancing age: "For some years after retiring I could not force myself to visit the works. This, alas, would recall so many who had gone before. Scarcely one of my early friends would remain to give me the hand-clasp of the days of old. Only one or two of these old men would call me 'Andy'" (279).

The *Autobiography* has been long held in high esteem, reprinted numerous times, and often assigned for reading in high schools and for college freshmen. Its simple, direct style, excellent choice of words, and smoothly flowing movement are exemplary. Its subject-matter and presentation are interesting to almost any type of reader. Its only serious fault is inaccuracy, and this is often unimportant except to the historian.

While its arrangement of materials is not always in the most desirable order, the complexity of the life Carnegie records is so great that anyone would find it difficult to order it better. Certainly none of the biographies of Carnegie in print have achieved any better arrangement.

From practically every point of view, literary, biographical or ideational, the *Autobiography* is Carnegie's best work. It would be interesting to know the style and content of the relatively large part which was excised by Van Dyke in editing the manuscript.

II *The Biography of James Watt*

When in 1904 the Edinburgh and London firm of Oliphant, Anderson and Ferrier sought someone to write a life of James Watt for its *Famous Scots* series, Carnegie was the obvious choice. An internationally known author and fellow Scot, he was also a titan of industry and well versed in the mechanical trades.

For some unspecified reason, his answer was a flat rejection, based on the multiplicity of his other interests. Then the old Carnegie curiosity made itself felt. Recalling that he knew little of Watt or of steam engine history, he felt that the necessity of writing would be his surest means of making up the gap in his knowledge. He offered to write the book, and in the preface reported these facts, happily adding: "I now know about the steam-engine, and have also had revealed to me one of the finest characters that ever graced the earth."[10]

In a sense Carnegie was indebted to Watt, "the creator of the most potent instrument of mechanical force known to man,"[11] even though his father's business was ruined by steam power. Carnegie writes: "The change from handloom to steam-loom weaving was disastrous to our family. My father did not recognize the impending revolution, and was struggling under the old system." But the same steam power that caused poverty in his early years later made possible his financial success—even to getting his first start in America running a steam-engine,[12] and later as a railroad official.

In dealing with his subject, Carnegie adopted a chronological order, commencing with the time and circumstances of the Scotsman's birth. From then on, the narrative flows smoothly with few digressions from the order of events. He did not encumber his writing with excessive, long passages dwelling on technical details concerning the numerous inventions of Watt. In contrast, James P. Muirhead, from whose work Carnegie evidently drew much of his material, emphasized the inventions of Watt and wrote in detail about them. Carnegie concentrated more on the man.

Carnegie, with his passion for lofty views, wrote: "Let the dreamers therefore dream on. The world, minus enchanting dreams, would be commonplace indeed, and let us remember this dream is only dreamable because Watt's steam-engine is a reality" (21).

Throughout the book one is apt to notice Carnegie's habit of personalizing words, such as "genius steam" (21), "pride of profession" (26), "demon steam" (34), "godlike reason" (45), "chariot of progress" and "fairy girdlist" (63). And all with a fine sense of the dramatic. For herein lay the heart of Carnegie's style. In one passage concerning the inventor's hitting upon an ingenious discovery Carnegie wrote: "Many plans were entertained, only to be finally rejected. At last the ₁ flash came into that teeming brain like a strike of lightning. Eureka! He had found it" (41).

As in his *Autobiography* Carnegie injects Shakespearean strains and other literary quotations into his biography of Watt. He writes: "We may picture him reciting in Falstaffian mood, 'Would my name were not so terrible to the enemy'" (87). Always Carnegie had a tendency to adapt quotations to situations: "For this is Coilantogle ford,/ And thou must keep thee with thy sword" (22).[13] As usual Carnegie gives no reference. Being very knowledgeable about folklore and literature he sometimes mentions an author's name, but usually seems to assume that the reader will recognize the quotation and know the source.

The familiar theme of devotion to his mother, so evident throughout Carnegie's *Autobiography*, frequently appears in his work on Watt. In writing about the inventor's mother, he often projects his own feelings into what he thought the relationship between Watt and his mother must have been, when in reality it was his own mother he obviously was writing about. According to Muirhead, Watt "received from his mother his first lessons in reading; his father taught him writing and arithmetic."[14] From this Carnegie embellishes: "She taught him to read most of what he then knew, and, we may be sure, fed him on the poetry and romance upon which she herself had fed, and for which he became noted in after life" (12). At first the reader is led to believe that he was tutored solely by his mother, although Carnegie does mention later that "his wise father not only taught him writing and arithmetic, but also provided a set of small tools for him" (14). Carnegie ignores the fact that Watt's father lost the family fortune in speculation.

Further reflecting upon the maternal theme, Carnegie notes: "For what a Scotch boy born to labour is to become, and how, cannot be forecast until we know what his mother is, who is to him nurse, servant, governess, teacher and saint, all in one" (9–10). And again the same refrain: "No school but one can instil that, where rules the one best teacher ... the school kept at your mother's knee. Such mothers as Watt had are the appointed trainers of genius, and make men good and great, if the needed spark be there to enkindle: 'Kings they make gods, and meaner subjects Kings'" (13). Nowhere in Muirhead's biography is there a hint of such high tribute to Watt's mother, although she was the writer's kinswoman, Agnes Muirhead.

Projecting his own feelings into those concerning the death of Watt's mother, Carnegie writes: "The relations between them had been such as are only possible between mother and son" (17).

Repeating the proverbial theme, "East or West, home is best," Carnegie says: "Watt never ceased to keep in close touch with his native town of Greenock and his Glasgow friends. His heart still warmed to the tartan, the soft, broad Scotch accent never forsook him; nor, we may be sure, did the refrain ever leave his heart" (85). In Carnegie's words: "The heather was on fire within Jamie's breast" (13). This fact alone would have kindled Carnegie's adoration for the man from the very start.

Hero-worship woven all through the biography manifests itself in passages such as this: "When the boy absorbs ... Wallace, the Bruce, and Sir John Graham, is fired by the story of the Martyrs, has at heart page after page of his country's ballads, and also, in more recent times, is at home with Burns's and Scott's prose and poetry, he has little room and less desire, and still less need, for the inferior heroes.... Self-seeking heroes passed in review without gaining admittance to the soul of Watt" (15–16). Sir Walter Scott, who also drank deep of Scottish lore, worshipped Watt as well. Carnegie quotes the words of the poet in reference to the inventor, "[Watt] was not only the most profound man of science, the most successful combiner of powers, and combiner of numbers, as adapted to practical purposes—was not only one of the most generally well informed, but one of the best and kindest of human beings" (158).

Carnegie's admiration of Watt is best expressed in the following passage: "Thou art the man; go up higher and take your seat there among the immortals, the inventor of the greatest of all inventions, a great discoverer, and one of the noblest of men!" (42).

In Watt's biography as well as his own life story Carnegie stresses the importance of frugal beginnings. About Watt Carnegie observes: "But the fates had been kind; for, burdened with neither wealth nor rank, this poor would-be skilled mechanic was to have a fair chance by beginning at the bottom among his fellows, the sternest yet finest of all schools to call forth and strengthen inherent qualities, and impel a poor young man to put forth his utmost effort when launched upon the sea of life, where he must either sink or swim, no bladders being in reserve for him" (21–22). And again: "There must be something in the soil which produces such men; something in the poverty that compels exertion" (135). Also: "Not from palace or castle, but from the cottage have come, or can come, the needed leaders of our race, under whose guidance it is to ascend" (9). And "...distinguished students, who figuratively speaking, cultivate knowledge upon a little oatmeal, earning money between terms to pay their way. It is highly probable that a greater proportion of these will be heard from in later years than of any other class" (30).

Here, too, Carnegie stresses the importance of trifles, as he did in his autobiography. He wrote: "Fortune sometimes hangs upon a glance or a nod of kindly recognition as we pass" (89).

Carnegie no doubt was projecting his own feelings into those of Watt when he wrote about satisfaction in honest work done: "It is highly probable that this first tool finished by his own hands brought to Watt more unalloyed pleasure than any of his greater triumphs of later years, just as the first week's wages of youth, money earned by service rendered, proclaiming coming manhood, brings with it a thrill and glow of proud satisfaction, compared with which all the millions of later years are as dross" (25). Carnegie had written in his autobiography the same sentiment: "I have made millions since, but none of those millions gave me such happiness as my first week's earnings."[15]

Another Carnegie theme which manifests itself in the biography of Watt is his desire for international peace and brotherhood. Borrowing from Tennyson and his Scottish hero, Burns, Carnegie writes: "We may continue, therefore, to indulge the hope of the coming 'parliament of man, the federation of the world.' . . . 'It's coming yet, for a' that, that man to man the warld o'er, shall brothers be for a' that' " (21), although it had no connection with Watt.

This Carnegie habit of pressing his own convictions upon others accounts for part of his description of his subject. Himself an enthusiastic fisherman, Carnegie infers that Watt was an avid angler: "The only 'sport' of the youth was angling, 'the most fitting practice for quiet men and lovers of peace,' the 'Brothers of the angle,' according to Izaak Walton, 'being mostly men of mild and gentle disposition' " (17).

Muirhead, on the other hand—and with close ties which gave him a better chance to know the facts—offers a far different conclusion. When a boy, he agrees, Watt often fished from a jetty at the back of his father's house on the shore at Greenock. It would be pleasant to think that he continued the sport in later life. "There would have been something cheerful in associating the name of James Watt with those of . . . Izaak Walton . . . and other eminent worthies" of the pastime.[16] But the evidence, he finds, is simply on the other side. Watt had neither the time, nor apparently the inclination to follow the sport. Carnegie must have overlooked, forgotten, or determinedly chosen to make his subject like and practice something so dear to himself.

Carnegie looked forward as well as back, in his treatment

of Watt. In reference to the scientist's discovery that water was a compound, instead of an element, he goes on: "Who shall doubt, after finding this secret source of force in water, that some future Watt is to discover other sources of power, or perchance succeed in utilizing the super-abundant power known to exist in the heat of the sun?" (39).

In the final analysis, Carnegie reflected his concern for old age and retirement as he did in his autobiography. It is interesting to note that when Carnegie wrote this, he was seventy years old. He laments: "The day had come when Watt awakened to one of the saddest of all truths, that his friends were one by one rapidly passing away, the circle ever narrowing" (143–44).

Carnegie's conclusion and summary again play up the subject as an inventor, a discoverer, and finally Watt—the man. In doing so, Carnegie, who always went to the most authoritative sources, quotes from others their opinions concerning Watt. He includes Henry P. Brougham, Humphry Davy, James Mackintosh, George Hamilton-Gordon, Francis Jeffrey, William T. Kelvin, and others (148–60).

III   *Stanton, Cornell, and Chambers Pamphlets*

Carnegie's other essays at biography were three memorial addresses on Edwin M. Stanton, Ezra Cornell, and William Chambers, later issued in pamphlet form. All are reprinted in *Miscellaneous Writings of Andrew Carnegie*, Volume I.[17]

In all three Carnegie uses some of his favorite themes: the advantages of poverty in youth, importance of family, interest in reading, fortunate chance, and influence of good women. It all sounds like a replay of Carnegie's own life.

The Stanton speech[18] is little more than a patriotic hurrah, wandering off into eulogy and a highly fantasized account of Stanton's part in the Civil War, which—Carnegie would make it appear—he won almost singlehandedly. Of course, Carnegie mentions how as a messenger boy he had come to know his subject, then a Pittsburgh attorney. If, as is probable, he had met either Cornell or Chambers, he fails to mention it in the speeches on them.

The Cornell address, delivered at Cornell University on

April 26, 1907, comes nearest to honest biography. Almost at the beginning he compares his subject to the inventor of the steam engine, asserting that he was, "like Watt . . . a decidedly mechanical genius." His own interest in women's rights—he and David McCargo were "the first to employ young women as telegraph operators in the United States upon railroads,"[19] and his uxorial devotion are reflected in his comment on the admission of young women to Cornell University: "Our country is generally credited with being in advance of others in this respect. Their presence and status here in Cornell and other universities give ground for this opinion. . . . In our day, man, and notably the American man, finds in his wife the angel leading him upward, both by precept and example, to higher and holier life, refining and elevating him, making his life purer and nobler."[20]

William Chambers[21] appealed to Carnegie as a fellow Scot, and, as with Cornell, a philanthropist and donor of libraries (210–11).

IV Related Materials

Six other related short compositions fall more or less within the realm of biography, but none of them really warrant the designation. They all lack vital statistics, background and other information which would enable the reader to reach any effective understanding of the life, thought, development and actions of the subject. Each is principally a momentary glimpse, little more.

The chapter "Characteristics" in the *Memoirs of Anne C. L. Botta*, New York, 1894, runs for six pages. It is mostly an account of Botta's kindness in introducing Carnegie, a green young Westerner in his mid-thirties, into the most cultivated society of New York. He tells of her parties, "nearest thing in the modern era to a real 'salon,'"[22] and the sadness at her funeral.

"Stevensonia," in *Critic*, January 12, 1895, is merely one of a number of brief tributes to Robert Louis Stevenson, the lament of a Scot for a fellow countryman.

Of somewhat more substance is "The Laird of Briarcliff," in the *Outlook* for May 16, 1898. It is a tribute to Walter W. Law, a New York merchant who retired from business at sixty, developing a large dairy and rose farm and establishing a model community for his employees. The pattern—son of poor Nonconformists; father an Independent and mother "of indomitable energy and enterprise," and Walter "her ain son"; put to work at fourteen; constant reader; friendly, hard working and aiding his family; youthful migrant to America; Horatio Alger type success, early retirement and philanthropy, sound almost as if Carnegie was writing about himself.

"Queen Victoria," a magazine article on the queen's death in 1901, and "William Ewart Gladstone," a memorial address at St. Deniol's Library on October 13, 1902, are mere bits of praise.

The untitled first of a group of "Tributes to Mark Twain," by prominent writers in *North American Review*, June 1910, is the best and most touching of the lot. Carnegie writes of his relationship with Clemens, and the humorist's honesty and acumen. It is a gem, but not biography.

V *Similarities of Carnegie, Watt, and Cornell*

It is a truism that one of the requirements for writing good biography is sympathy with the subject.[23] Carnegie qualified in this respect to write about both Watt and Cornell. Perhaps one reason why he became so enthusiastic about each one was the number of shared similar experiences. The adage "Like draws to like," which he quoted from time to time, well applies in regard to his admiration for each of the two.

Watt and Carnegie were born in Scotland, within fifteen months of a century apart, and died within eight days of the same period. Cornell's life spanned the gap between the pair, being contemporary with the inventor for twelve years and with the steelman for thirty-seven. All three came of good families reduced to near poverty, the Carnegies by technological change, the Cornells by business failure, and the Watts by speculation.

None of the three had more than a meager common-school education except for what he received from his family and what he later obtained by individual study. All were lifelong students, widely known for practical or scientific attainments, and became acquainted with and respected by most of the principal men of their nation and period.

Each left his birthplace when very young (Cornell and Watt at eighteen) and made his own way in strange surroundings. Cornell moved half across New York state, Carnegie to America, and Watt to England. Carnegie and Watt both suffered from ill health and repeatedly returned to Scotland on this account. Carnegie wrote: "To the old home in Scotland our hero's face was now turned in the autumn of 1756, his twentieth year.[24] His native air, best medicine of all for the invalid exile, soon restored his health."[25] In regard to himself he had written: "The cool highland air has been to me a panacea for many years. My physician has insisted that I must avoid our hot American summers."[26]

Both Carnegie and Watt had mechanical genius assistants on whom they relied and in whom they placed complete trust. For Carnegie it was Capt. William Jones and for Watt, William Murdock. Carnegie wrote: "An American Murdock was found in Captain Jones, the best manager of works of his day.... Fortunate is the firm that discovers a William Murdock or William Jones, and gives him swing to do the work of an original in his own way."[27]

All three men became philanthropists on an unexpected scale for their times. Carnegie and Cornell both endowed universities, and each donated a library to his home town. Carnegie and Cornell both built railways, and Watt designed engines for railway use. All three married happily and all were ahead of their times in regard to religion, Carnegie noted: "It seems probable that Watt, in his theological views . . . was in advance of his age." "The cry was raised that [Cornell] intended to establish a Godless University." "Those who hold today that the Sabbath in its fullest sense was made for man . . . are not more advanced than were my parents forty years ago."[28]

Carnegie and Cornell planned early retirement from business, the latter attaining his aim at about fifty. Carnegie, as he noted of Watt, "gracefully glided into old age. This is the great test of success in life," he added.[29] All three died of pneumonia.

VI   *Evaluation*

Literarily, Carnegie was less successful in his essays at biography than in any of his other writing. The *Autobiography*, although a classic of simple prose, is poorly organized and contains many factual errors. The Watt biography, although internationally published and reprinted several times, shows little knowledge of the background material. It contains far too much identification of author and subject, as can be said of the Cornell speech and those on Chambers and Stanton. Most modern writers on these men simply ignore Carnegie's work. And while few biographers of Carnegie have shown any tendency to question the *Autobiography* on matters of fact or interpretation,[30] those who have followed it closely have often been led into error by the practice.

Only in the *Autobiography* does Carnegie achieve the canon that biography should be "... interpretive, whether of real people, of actual events or of ideas."[31] In his other essays in the field he completely misses the aim that in "great biography ... it is the personality of the subject rather than his achievements that has made the book great."[32] He constantly violates the rule that a good biographer must keep himself in the background.[33] The one saving grace in them all is what Elizabeth Nitchie calls the crowning virtue of style in biography—simplicity.[34]

Perhaps Carnegie's principal difficulty in the field was that he never really understood biography. Travel he knew; politics and economics he learned; letter writing came to him naturally, as did journalism, which to him was a branch of the same field; and he studied assiduously to become an interesting and forceful speaker. But biography to him was never more than praise for someone he admired—including himself. That is why his one acceptable essay in the field was the *Autobiography*, whose subject he understood, even if he confused times, circumstances and other facts. *James Watt*, the Chambers, Stanton, and Cornell pamphlets, and "The Laird of Briarcliff Manor" were largely produced by putting himself into the shoes of his subjects.

CHAPTER 9

Man of Letters: 1849-1915

AN inveterate letter writer, Carnegie seems to have had a pen in hand at all times, despite the overwhelmingly active life he led. Even after he had become internationally known as a prominent figure, he wrote constantly to his family, friends, business associates, to newspapers, and public figures, including five presidents with whom he was on friendly terms.

Unfortunately, no considerable collection of his letters has ever been published, although many of them are quoted, in whole or in part, in the Wall and Hendrick biographies, and scores appeared in newspapers to whose editors he directed them.

Throughout his letter writing, from the very beginning, Carnegie used an abbreviated style. He employed the ampersand most of the time and frequently capitalized nouns and words for emphasis according to old style. In 1903 Carnegie's staccato, telegraphic style with little punctuation became exaggerated, for it was at this time that he had endowed the Simplified Spelling Board. However, by 1915 he became discouraged due to lack of progress in his revolution of the English language. He wrote, "I think I hav been patient enuf. . . . I hav a much better use for twenty-five thousand dollars a year."[1]

But to himself he remained true. Carnegie continued to the end in his correspondence to use this abbreviated form, and even if he slipped and forgot to simplify, he would carefully erase "have" and rewrite it as "hav," in order to be consistent.

I Family Letters

As a youth, soon after his arrival in America, Carnegie began a trans-Atlantic correspondence with the Lauders—usually writing to his uncle, George Lauder, and cousin, George, Jr., more affectionately called "Dod." His letters were informative, keeping the Scottish relatives up to date on the family's progress, and what was happening in the New World. After a few years he began using the correspondence to debate differences in British and American ideas and political systems.

In later years he corresponded continually with his mother and brother Tom, whenever they were apart, and with Tom's widow, Lucy Coleman Carnegie, as well as with Louise Whitfield during their courtship. Following their marriage they were seldom apart for any length of time. A typical family letter is that written from Parma, Italy, on December 14, 1865, during the walking tour of Europe.[2] The letter is a good example of its kind, part business, part news, and with a reserved expression of sentiment, although he often addressed his brother somewhat as an inferior, in the manner of a superior talking to a subordinate, or at least, an older sibling giving his "kid brother" advice.

A previous letter, mailed just before the writing of this one, had recognized that business conditions were very bad, and expressed an intention of returning home in a month with Henry Phipps, who was cutting his part of the trip short, and expected to be home to Pittsburgh by the end of January. But Carnegie had just been reassured by a letter from Tom.

He opens this letter abruptly by explaining that with a new turn of events he feels no necessity for disappointing other members of the party by walking out on them. But he is willing to return if necessary:

> I just feel this way about it—twenty Italys wouldn't keep me if my brother was having too much anxiety about matters. I feel that very few persons of your years have ever had such a load to travel under. I don't know anyone, I'm sure, whom I would consider able for such a task.

Carnegie expresses a hope that this letter will overtake the previous one, to avoid causing Tom unnecessary concern.

Switching to family matters, he asks for a picture of Lucy, and suggests that her father, who is to occupy the new Carnegie home until spring, handle arrangements for putting in a furnace.

He joshes about the news that a mutual friend is getting married: "Your item about John Hampton almost took the breath from me. If he goes, who is safe? I shall henceforth esteem myself not invulnerable." The letter closes with friendly chatter about how he will tease their mother on returning home. It is a cheerful, informal missive.

II *Letters to Friends*

In writing to his friends, many of whom were business associates or public figures, Carnegie was flippant at times, calling them "pard" or "chum" throughout his letters. It is obvious that even with his friends he did not mince words. While continually giving prophetic advice or pep talks, he pressed his convictions upon others.

At times he was blunt. In corresponding with British friends he spared no feelings, and warned them vehemently on differences in national policies. He wrote long, earnest letters, lecturing and preaching, with poetic effusions (quoted). When his own feelings were hurt, he would write in the suffering tones of a martyr. But when a friend expressed such feelings, he nipped self-pity in the bud.

A good example of his style is his letter to Herbert Spencer of January 5, 1897,[3] in reply to one of December 16, from Brighton.[4] Spencer had been approached on the subject of receiving public honors, and indicated he planned to refuse the gesture because of long previous neglect. Carnegie's letter, a classic of its kind, opens with New Year's greetings and closes with brief personal matters. The intervening five paragraphs are all designed to cheer up the gloomy old friend by spanking him gently.

I hope you will reconsider the whole matter, and come to the conclusion that the greater the neglect shown by your fellow countrymen, the higher the tribute to what you laid before them. . . . When have the Prophets not been stoned, from Christ down to Wagner? . . .

Why, my dear friend, what do you mean by complaining of neglect, abuse, scorn? These are the precious rewards of the teachers of mankind. The Poets fare no better. . . .

I could wish that you had been imprisoned, tortured on the rack.

This would have been no greater reward than is your due. The Philosopher who is sensitive to contemporaneous criticism is a new type, and I do not wish you to pass into history as its founder.

Carnegie urges his friend to do away with anything he has written which shows "other than a spirit of deep gratification at the neglect, scorn and abuse which you have had to suffer." The proper attitude, he urges, should be that of "lofty pity and anxiety for their reaching the light by and by, which you have discovered and in which you rest. . . ."

Referring to their early meeting,[5] he warns the philosopher: "The "Cheddar vs Cheshire" cheese story will pass into history, and prove that you are not altogether a "Brooding God" but something also of the human. But, my belief is, that one word showing disappointment, or, may I say, resentment, of the treatment you have received from your countrymen, will detract very much from the loftiness of our Guide, Philosopher and Friend." Then he closes the letter with a bit of friendly chatter having no relation to the subject of his admonition.

III *Business Letters*

The business letters of Andrew Carnegie were ordinarily (but not invariably) brief and to the point. Sometimes he opened with staggering abruptness, as in the first letter he wrote to the trustees of the Peace Fund: "I have transferred to you as trustees . . . $10,000,000 of five-per-cent first mortgage bonds, value $11,500,000, the revenue of which is to be administered by you to hasten the abolition of international war, the foulest blot upon our civilization."[6]

A typical Carnegie business letter—except for the content—and a good one considering the situation, was that written to John G. A. Leishman on December 24, 1894.[7] Leishman, a partner who had been promoted to chief executive of Carnegie Steel on the resignation of Frick, was discovered to have been speculating in pig iron, a practice Carnegie considered inexcusable. Henry Phipps had passed the word along just before the letter was written. On learning the situation, Carnegie wrote as much in sorrow for an old friend as in anger:

Dear Mr. Leishman:

You have made tomorrow a sorry Christmas for me and for Mr. Phipps from whom I have heard. You have not treated me fairly as your partner. You know I often congratulated you on your *not* speculating in pig, and upon the fact that we were clear of purchases beyond this year. You kept silence and deluded me. You deceived your partner and friend, and only kept faith with him when you could deceive him no longer.

It is not the loss of money caused by your conduct, for it is better to lose than gain by speculation; neither the fact that you have involved me in speculation, which I consider dishonorable, although this hurts as you well know, but that you should have concealed our position—deceived your partner—*that* is what shakes my confidence and renders me so unhappy. What I ever did to tempt you to other than straightforward dealing with me, I cannot imagine.

I have been deceived by one whom I trusted—by a partner and a friend; do what I will, thinking over my conduct to this friend I can find nothing to justify such treatment from him.

After signing the letter, Carnegie added a postscript: "This will not be sent until your Christmas day is over. I would make it less sad than mine." The situation was patched up for a time, but almost exactly two years later Carnegie removed Leishman from his position for a similar breach of ethics.[8] Years later, however, after Leishman had lost his fortune, Carnegie placed him upon a personal pension for life.[9]

Charming as Carnegie's letters to friends might be, he was at his best when angry. Winkler quotes from instructions to Charles M. Schwab at the time that certain rival companies backed by J. Pierpont Morgan had formed a combination to control the ferrous metals trade—the situation that eventuated in Morgan's purchase of Carnegie's holdings. In part, the letter ran: "In the case of this ... Company as in the case of the American Wire Company, if our president steps forward at the right time and in the right way, informs these people that we do not propose to be injured, on the contrary, we expect to reap great gains from it; that we will observe an *armed neutrality* as long as it is made to our interest to do so, but that we require this arrangement—then specify what is advantageous for us, very advantageous, more advantageous than existed before the combination and he will get it. If they decline to give us what we want, then there must be no bluff. We must accept the situation and prove that if it is fight they want, here we are 'always ready.' Here is a historic situation for the Managers to study—Richelieu's advice: 'First, all means to conciliate; failing that, all means to crush.' ... We should look with favor upon every combination of every kind on the part of our competitors; the bigger they grow the more vulnerable they become."

IV *Letters to Public Figures*

For most of his last thirty years, Carnegie carried on a voluminous correspondence with many of the world's most prominent men, including presidents of the United States, prime ministers and secretaries of state, and even King Edward VII of England and Kaiser Wilhelm II of Germany.

With the highest public officials and other important men, his style and attitude were much the same as usual. Although he always addressed a chief executive as "Mr. President," Carnegie said exactly what he felt. Being on intimate terms with Cleveland, McKinley, Theodore Roosevelt, Taft, and Wilson, he exercised a strong influence, and often took a hand at running the government indirectly.

Carnegie's style of writing became even more forceful in age than it had been in earlier years. His words were intense and impatient at times as he became increasingly devoted to the cause of peace. Even with those in the highest positions, Carnegie did not hesitate to scold, command and at times threaten, in order to get his way.

One of the most interesting letters of this type is that addressed to the Kaiser on January 19, 1907,[10] when it appeared likely that the Emperor was preparing to block the proposed Hague conference. Far from his characteristic style, Carnegie wrote in a manner reminiscent of his 1904 magazine article, "Britain's Appeal to the Gods."[11] The missive was in two parts, the first a brief, two paragraph introduction, the other a supposed daydream sequence. Altogether, it is a most remarkable communication, written persuasively and with great charm, well planned and organized.

The letter proper, or opening part, after the salutation, begins abruptly: "In my reveries you sometimes appear and enter my brain. I then imagine myself 'The Emperor' and soliloquize somewhat as per enclosed." This is simply followed by a polite closing, varying from usual custom only in its ending: "and with profound interest in your 'Star,' which should excel all others in brilliancy if followed boldly."

The "enclosure" also opens abruptly: "The august visitor, 'The Emperor,' communes with himself thus when I am transformed:—"

Here, speaking for the Emperor, Carnegie writes in the first person. "God has seen fit to place me in command of the greatest military power ever known." Surely this is to produce good, not evil. "Thank God, my hands *as yet*, are guiltless of human blood," he continues after reflecting on the difference between the heroes of barbarism and civilization. Perhaps God has destined him to bring peace to the world.

The reverie goes on to consider the international situation, the Kaiser's opportunity, climaxing: "Yes! This is my work! Thank God. Now I see my path and am happy. To this I consecrate my life, and surely, 'The highest Worship of God is service to man.'"

At this point Carnegie wakes and becomes himself again, "but still I keep wishing that I were indeed the Emperor and had his part to play." He again lays out the Kaiser's opportunity, in new words and phrases. In conclusion, he points out that if the President had the power to take such action, Carnegie would "have been at his side long ago, urging it." Roosevelt's part will be played well, "*and for Peace, too*—but there is only one on earth to whom has been given the power to resolve and execute—the Emperor of Germany. Pitiable will be his place in history should he falter. 'Where much is given much is required.'"

After holding the letter for four days, he dispatched it through the American ambassador, Charlemagne Tower, with an offer to visit and talk with Wilhelm if so desired. Apparently Tower showed this letter, too, to the Kaiser, for on their meeting that worthy commented on a phrase in the missive to Tower: "He and our President would make a team if they were only hitched up together for the great cause of Peace."[12] In the *Autobiography*,[13] describing the week he spent at Kiel, and his talks with the Emperor, Carnegie quotes the Kaiser: "Oh, I see! You wish to drive us together. Well, I agree if you make Roosevelt first horse I shall follow." Carnegie's reply was, "Ah, no, Your Majesty, I know horse-flesh better than to attempt to drive two such gay colts tandem.... I must yoke you both in the shafts, neck and neck, so I can hold you in."

Wilhelm was friendly and gave Carnegie a good hearing— perhaps even considered his suggestion seriously. It would be interesting to know whether, during his years as a virtual prisoner in Holland, the exiled emperor ever recalled the accuracy of Carnegie's prediction as to his place in history "if he should falter."

V *Letters to Newspapers*

Very early in life Carnegie discovered the power of the press, and was deeply impressed by the opportunity it offered for one individual in a democracy to influence a situation. Success with his first letter to a newspaper, promoting Col. Anderson's library as being free to all working boys,[14] encouraged him to continue writing to editors, sometimes bitterly, always with argument, and often letters full of advice and counsel.

Beginning with missives to his home-town papers in Pittsburgh, he enlarged his field as time passed, and his influence widened. During the final thirty years of his active career he wrote frequently and at considerable length to the principal dailies of the United States, and many of those in England and Scotland as well. Apparently most of these letters were published, even those addressed argumentatively to editors in opposition to their views. He argued for causes, disputed with other writers, answered criticisms and not infrequently predicted the course of events.

Around the turn of the century Carnegie began sending New Year's greetings and warning or encouraging forecasts to newspapers around the holiday season. One of these, less than five years before his death, is a good example of his press letters. In answer to a request, he wrote to the editor of the *Pittsburgh*

Dispatch, in which his letter was printed on January 1, 1915. Writing on "America's Opportunity," his argument is: 1. America has no enmities nor rivalries for materials; 2. this happy situation results from friendly national policies; 3. she needs no large armaments or military forces; 4. there is no reason for anything but optimism in regard to the nation's future.

This letter is worth quoting almost in full, as an example of Carnegie's crisp, sententious style and optimistic nationalism, varying little from the correspondence he had carried on with Dod more than half a century earlier:

Thanks for your kind favor in which you suggest that I say a few words upon "America's Opportunity."

First: Our beloved Republic has no enemies in the world, neither personal nor national. She covets no new territory and wishes all nations peace and prosperity, setting an example to all the world. She is the foremost of nations in longing for international peace, knowing that "Peace hath her victories much more renowned than those of war."[15]

Immigrants come to her from many nations, all certain of being classed under the laws of our own citizens. She welcomes all, and shares her privileges with them. In due time, these arrivals apply for citizenship and become Americans—one man's privilege, every citizen's right—their children educated at our schools, free of expense. She is the pioneer nation proclaiming the brotherhood of man.

She needs no increase in army or navy. The latter is today quite sufficient, better that it were not so large; and as for the army— 16,000,000 militia, subject to call, and if called to repel invaders, our only difficulty would be to provide for the surplus millions who would report. Men who advocate increased armies for us can be likened only to those who are afraid to step out of their homes without a lightning rod down their backs, because men have been known to be struck by lightning. Our Republic has nothing to fear, our march is onward and upward. She leads the procession, other nations must follow.

As Wall comments: "Any one of his letters to Cousin Dod, written when he was fifteen, sixty-five years before, could have been substituted for this letter, and no one would have known the difference."[16]

CHAPTER 10

Fair-Haired Scotch Angel: 1901-1919

FOR three decades after the chosen time,[1] Andrew Carnegie was unable to carry out his plan to retire from active business and devote his life to culture, politics, and philanthropy. There is no reason to question his intention. But as years passed, business matters became more and more complex, and he felt compelled to protect the best interests of partners and employees, for all of whom—despite the fiasco of the Homestead steel strike—he retained a paternal feeling. In a letter to Samuel Storey, January 3, 1883, during his newspaper venture, he said, "I am going out of business but it takes a little more time than I had bargained for—that's all."[2]

In 1899 a group led by Henry C. Frick tried to buy the Carnegie holdings for $175 million. Carnegie was willing, but the deal fell through for lack of backing, and he pocketed over $1 million in option money.[3] When J. P. Morgan proposed a major merger two years later through Charles M. Schwab, Carnegie immediately accepted, opening the way for the formation of United States Steel Corporation. He declined to remain a partner, taking as his share about $300 million in 5 percent gold bonds. These were placed in a specially built vault in Hoboken, N.J., as Carnegie never wanted to see or touch any of them.[4]

Freed from the concerns of manufacturing, on which—despite his capable officers and long absences—he had always kept a sharp watch, Carnegie turned his mind to the things he had been anticipating for so long. His self-education had replaced the plan to study at Oxford, and his newspaper venture was far behind him. There remained his writing (which by this time had become one of his best-loved activities) and his philanthropies.

His literary output continued about as usual, both in volume and subject matter, although with a slight decrease in magazine articles for the first five years. Two of the three published in 1901 appeared before the sale of his business was final,[5] and the third may have been under way, as it appeared in the June issue of *Nineteenth Century*. But in 1902 he published *The Empire of Business*—a collection of his previous articles and speeches—and had two speeches printed and two articles published. From 1903 there are at least nine pamphlet speeches, all dealing with his philanthropies, but in the following year a single magazine article, on international affairs. In 1905 came his one full-scale biography, *James Watt*, one speech, and one article. With 1906 his writing activity was again at full steam, with four articles; the next year two pamphlet speeches, three magazine articles and a book introduction.[6] His articles, except for an increased emphasis on philanthropy and peace, differed little from his previous style.

I   A Remarkable Introduction

The year 1908 brought his last book, *Problems of Today*, four articles, and an introduction to *The Roosevelt Policy*.[7] When a well-known publishing company decided to issue a two-volume edition of Theodore Roosevelt's addresses, state papers and letters on the control of corporate wealth and the relation of capital and labor, Andrew Carnegie was a natural choice to introduce it.

That "Introduction"[8] is a remarkable piece of work. Although Carnegie was in his seventy-second year when he wrote it, the thinking is as clear and the writing as crisp as if he had been many years younger. The thirteen-page (approximately 5,000-word) essay is no puff, although it speaks highly of Roosevelt. Instead it points out that the book is devoted not to the man, but to his policies. Neither does it attempt to set up arguments against those positions with which the philanthropist disagreed.

Carnegie opens with a brief assessment of the President as a man of destiny, and the times which called for such a man. He details what he considers Roosevelt's characteristics in meeting such situations, and concludes with a question which was being widely asked by thinking men.

Roosevelt like Lincoln, Carnegie points out, is a man with peculiarities beyond the usual expectation. "He would not be original if he were like anybody else. None but himself can be his parallel. . . . Talent can be hammered into shape and conform itself to social conventions. . . . With genius this is impossible—one of the marked differences between talent and genius being that talent does what it can, genius what it must" (ix).

After a century of unparalleled industrial growth in which the nation's energies had been directed to the development of its resources, legislation to safeguard public interest had been neglected. Particularly during the thirty years following the Civil War almost free rein had been given to this type of expansion on a scale never before approached by any nation. "There came the serious task of regulating interstate commerce and restricting the powers of trusts and corporations which threatened the structure of good government itself. It was at this crisis Roosevelt appeared upon the scene and became immediately a leader in the crusade,—in his gubernatorial message to the State of New York in 1899, just nine years ago. From that day to this he has hammered away and descanted always upon the same lines" (x).

After citing a dozen of the messages and papers dealing with such matters Carnegie briefly outlines Roosevelt's positions on the other principal matter involved, the relation of capital and labor (x–xi). Seeking the source of his subject's energy, he finds it in a paper, "Conduct as the Ultimate Test of Religious Belief," although wondering how the President managed to harmonize it with "the Scottish Covenanting strain in him." But Carnegie feels that all Americans are debtors to Roosevelt's teaching when he tells Christians that "more and more people who possess either religious belief, or aspiration after it, are growing to demand conduct as the ultimate test of the worth of belief" (xii).

Carnegie points out Roosevelt's principal innovations including the creation of a new cabinet post (Secretary of Commerce and Labor), pure food laws and conservation of natural resources, on which he had just called the first Governors Conference. "He reminds one of the description given of the first Naysmith steam hammer, as cracking a nut or forging an anchor with equal facility.... The heavier the blow required, the better ... the busiest man in the world ... is surely the President" (xiii–xiv). Roosevelt, he continues, has accomplished wonders in the field of commerce, both interstate and corporate. Citing the statement of Elbert H. Gary, president of the United States Steel Corporation, that the president's principles had "increased my feeling of responsibility toward the stockholders I represent, toward our competitors, toward business men, and toward the public" (xv), Carnegie cites Roosevelt's almost unerring choice of men to be appointed to important positions, then looks into the future:

When the day comes, as come it will, history is to record that just as Washington, struggling for Constitutional Rights, led the hosts that ensured national independence, as Lincoln preserved the Union by uprooting the sole cause of disunion, so will stand Roosevelt, who brought order out of chaos in our Interstate Commerce, and in our industrial system elevated and purified the conceptions of fiduciary duty in men of affairs, investigated charges and sternly enforced honesty in the dealings of officials, enforcing everywhere a stricter rule of conduct and a higher standard of action than that which before his day had unfortunately prevailed. More than this will the true historian add if he speaks the whole truth: namely, that the President also lived up to the high standard he set for others. (xx)

In conclusion, Carnegie quotes John Morley: "I have seen two wonders in America, Roosevelt and Niagara." He continues:

Niagara will run its course and so will Roosevelt, but both are fresh and overflowing.... He would be a bold man who attempted to forecast the future of either. Roosevelt's policy is already victorious.... The Presidency may be held by another ... but strip him of all external dignities and there still remains the Man in full possession of marvelous powers, high ideals, sleepless activity and boundless popularity.... Is he to sigh for more worlds to conquer and, after a rest, to reappear among the champions, eager for the fray, or to forsake public life and rust in inaction? The Sybil is silent. (xxi)

Quite unexpectedly, the "Introduction," something seldom read, created a sensation. One journal, at least, gave it more space in its review than it did to all the rest of the work.[9] The reviewer expressed surprise that a book attacking the undue concentration of wealth "should be sent" into the world with an introductory benediction from one of the two richest men in America. "But Mr. Carnegie, as we all know, has always been 'on the side of the angels,' and the reformers." The praise was due to Carnegie's personal admiration for Roosevelt, and agreement with some of the policies. As he was to demonstrate later the same year in *Problems of Today*,[10] his belief in the necessity of large fortunes had not changed.

From 1909 we have one pamphlet speech, 1910 two magazine articles, and in 1911 five, with a speech which was published the following year. From this time on—he was seventy-six years old—his output dropped, but before his production ceased there were five more articles, two in 1914, and one each in 1913, 1915 and 1916. Work on the *Autobiography*, published after his death, continued until the onset of World War I in 1914.

II   *The Business of Philanthropy*

During these years, however, Carnegie considered philanthropy his principal work. Having amassed the world's largest private fortune, he wanted to use it while he lived. As early as 1887 he had told William E. Gladstone he considered it a disgrace to die rich.[11] Carnegie felt that at his age the major task would be enough—to disperse wisely what he already had accumulated. He underestimated the stupendous job ahead of him, and later stated that he had not worked one-tenth as hard in acquiring his fortune as he did in divesting himself of his great wealth.[12]

In his autobiography Carnegie wrote, "as usual, Shakespeare had placed his talismanic touch upon the thought and framed the sentence—'So distribution should undo excess, and each man have enough.' "[13]

His main goal was not for charitable relief, holding that this was the responsibility of the State, and often did more harm than good, but instead for the promotion of education which would help to prevent poverty and ignorance. During his lifetime, Carnegie gave over 80 percent of his fortune for educational purposes of one kind or another. To him the mind was the greatest wealth, and he set about to stimulate all those he could reach.

By 1919, Carnegie had donated 7689 organs to churches throughout the world—his first going in 1873 to the Swedenborgian Church of his father.[14]

Libraries were early in his mind. Believing that "the chief glory of a nation is its authors,"[15] Carnegie saved the library of Lord Acton (the greatest historical student in England) by buying it himself in 1890, and putting the former owner in charge. Through his efforts it finally went to Cambridge University in 1902.[16] Carnegie considered libraries his specialty and by the time of his death had given 2811 free public library buildings to English-speaking countries.[17]

Contrary to common belief, Carnegie did not require or encourage these institutions to bear his name. In his words, "I do not wish to be remembered for what I gave, but for that which I have persuaded others to give."[18] By building libraries, he inspired communities to fill them with books, asking only that they inscribe the words "Let there be light" above the entrance.[19]

Although Carnegie had in 1885 given $50,000 to establish the first great medical research laboratory in the United States at Bellevue Hospital in New York, and had at the same time sent four children at his own expense to Paris to be treated by Louis Pasteur for rabies, he did not do much medical financing. He contended that this was John D. Rockefeller's specialty. However, he did make a $120,000 donation to the Koch Institute of Berlin for medical research and gave $50,000 to Madame Curie for her work in radiology. And due to his wife's interest in Helen Keller, he contributed to the New York and Massachusetts associations for the blind.[20]

Even these benefactions did not satisfy Carnegie's philanthropic nature, and he began to distribute his wealth with more zeal, concentrating most of his efforts within the years from 1901 to 1911. Soon his headquarters in the mansion house at No. 2 East Ninety-First and Fifth Avenue, New York, became one of the most famous of all American addresses. During these years he literally received mail in bushel baskets with requests for money from all over the world. One story is told of a gentleman asking timidly for a meager $5,000. Carnegie declined, asserting, "I am not interested in the retail business!"[21]

Starting with the men in his former mills, Carnegie established a $4 million pension and relief fund, also donating a million dollars to maintain the libraries and halls he had built for the workmen. These lines, written in 1903, from the workers at Homestead, express most feelingly the sentiment inspired by his action: "The interest which you have always shown in your workmen has won for you an appreciation which cannot be expressed by mere words. . . . We have personal knowledge of cares lightened and of hope and strength renewed in homes where human prospects seemed dark and discouraging."[22]

As early as 1881 Carnegie offered Pittsburgh $250,000 for a library and concert hall. The offer was refused, and he made the gift to Allegheny City—now Pittsburgh's North Side. About the time the library was dedicated in 1890, Pittsburgh asked him to renew the offer. He gave $1 million, later increased many times over, to include a museum and art gallery. He also provided for a craft school for workmen, which in 1912 became a college, and is now Carnegie-Mellon University.[23]

In 1904 his second large gift was incorporated in Washington, D.C.—to promote knowledge in all universities of the United States. This Carnegie Institution was valued then at $25 million, and was the least criticized of all of Carnegie's endowments.[24]

Steeped in a lifetime of hero worship, Carnegie's next gift—his dream of a world-wide Hero Fund—soon materialized. This brain-child and pet fund was inspired mainly by the heroic but futile rescue effort in which a former Pittsburgh mine superintendent and others lost their lives at the time of the Harwick disaster in 1904. The $5 million fund, established in America in 1904, was later extended to the Carnegie Fund Trust for Great Britain and Canada, and eventually, similar ones in France, Germany, Italy, Belgium, Holland, Norway, Sweden, Switzerland and Denmark.[25]

Since Carnegie believed that the teaching profession was underpaid, he established in 1905 what he considered his fourth most important gift—The Carnegie Foundation for the Advancement of Teaching—a $15 million pension plan which organized the Teacher's Insurance and Annuity Association of America in 1917.[26]

To his native Scotland Carnegie gave $10 million in 1901 toward education—half of which was to be used to pay the fees of deserving poor students and the other half for the improvement of universities. This endowment, known as the Carnegie Trust for the Universities of Scotland, met with much opposition—one of the most controversial of all his large benefactions. Carnegie did not anticipate the bitter criticism he would encounter as a result of his philanthropy. The public thought he was doing too much.[27]

Carnegie believed that the smaller institutions and colleges were in greater need of help and preferred to concentrate on them. To Princeton, disillusioned and thinking it would receive a good portion of the Carnegie money, he gave a lake for the promotion of a rowing crew to take the young men's minds off football, a sport to which Carnegie had an aversion. The sage was not without humor, even when it came to giving. By the time of his death he had distributed $27 million among 500 institutions of learning.[28]

III *Purchasing Peace*

International peace being foremost in his mind all his life, it was only natural that Carnegie would do great services in its behalf. Along with the Hero Fund, which was intended to point out that peace as well as war had heroes, there was his attempt to revolutionize the English language, establishing The Simplified Spelling Board in 1903 for the benefit of world-wide communication which he assumed would ultimately lead to peace. This project was made sport of by humorists and the press, who ridiculed him by employing his own reasoning, spelling his name "Androo Karnage." After donating $25,000 a year toward the fund until 1915, Carnegie finally gave up this endeavor.[29]

Thinking that money could buy anything, Carnegie built three temples of peace—the Pan American Union Building opened in 1910 in Washington, D. C.; another in Cartago, Costa Rica, dedicated the same year and named the Central American Court of Justice; and the third, which was begun first, finished last and caused the most problems (1907–1913)—The Temple of Peace, at The Hague. Together with these he endowed four trusts between 1903 and 1914 for the cause of peace totaling $25,250,000.[30] In 1914 he gave over $2 million to the Church Peace Union.[31]

Among his other important benefactions were: $10 million to the Carnegie United Kingdom Trust in 1913; $1,500,000 to the United Engineering Society; $850,000 to the International Bureau of American Republics; $2,500,000 during war years to the Red Cross, YMCA, and Knights of Columbus; and sums ranging from $100,000 to $500,000 to a score of research hospitals and educational boards.[32]

The world in general places its value and emphasis on the great benefactions already mentioned, but to Carnegie himself two others gave the most satisfaction. First was his private pension fund. There was never any publicity regarding the anonymous recipients. Only Carnegie and his intimate friends knew of the gifts that were given to others in this category. At the end of his life Carnegie was distributing $250,000 a year among almost five hundred beneficiaries.[33]

The gift which probably delighted him most of all was a historic and personal triumph—giving Pittencrieff Glen to the townspeople of Dunfermline. By this time Carnegie had already given a library to his native town (1881), $25,000 for swimming baths (1873), and the Carnegie Dunfermline Trust of $4 million (1903). The community with a population of 27,000 had the largest per capita private endowment in the world as a result of Carnegie benefactions.[34]

But the park pleased him more than anything—an air-castle that indeed came true. He wrote in his *Autobiography*, "Pittencrieff Glen is the most soul-satisfying gift I ever made, or ever can make."[35] Carnegie as a youth was barred from viewing the historic ruins of Malcolm's Tower, Margaret's Shrine, and the last remains of the palace of the Stuarts, due to a feud between his grandfather Morrison and the landowner. The eccentric James Hunt decreed that no Morrison or descendant of a Morrison should "ever step foot on Pittencrieff's sacred soil." Carnegie bought the entire property in 1902, and gave it to the town the following year, retaining only a small portion, including Malcolm's Tower—the birthplace of Scottish history. Thus Carnegie became the Laird of Pittencrieff of the Royal Berg of Dunfermline.[36] A fantastic storybook ending, Carnegie loving every morsel of drama, romance, and sense of climactic outcome.

IV *Fun in Giving*

At first Carnegie considered it a game to give his money away. Whereas most men enjoyed making money, he in contrast delighted in seeing his fortune diminish. There never lived a man who had as much fun in giving away his wealth as Carnegie. One of his teasing tricks in giving was to hold his beneficiary in suspense, using the element of surprise. While playing golf with Sir Swire Smith one day in 1899, Carnegie offered to give him a stroke a hole. Later that evening Smith mentioned Keighley Institute in their conversation. Carnegie asked if there was a library in the English town. When the answer was in the negative, he asked if $50,000 would be enough, and his partner was overcome with joy. The next morning during another round of golf Carnegie said, "I have repented of the offer I made you yesterday." Smith was crest-fallen until Carnegie added, "I don't think, after all, I can give you a stroke a hole!"[37]

In 1905 Carnegie again became involved in politics, both domestic and foreign, and this took much of his time away from philanthropy. By 1906 he was tired of the game of distribution and by 1910 completely disgusted. He had to abandon his "Gospel of Wealth" as too arduous an undertaking. No longer believing that one man was capable of disposing of such a fortune, he resigned the task to the discretion of others.

Discouraged, he realized that he could not give his money away fast enough. As Wall states, "The interest on his bonds kept gaining on his dispersal of those bonds. He had given away $180,000,000 but he still had almost the same amount left." Finally in 1911 Carnegie established and gave $125 million—the bulk of his fortune—to the Carnegie Corporation of New York for the advancement of knowledge, giving freedom to the trustees on how to spend it.[38] Carnegie, with utmost modesty, never even mentioned this largest contribution of all in his *Autobiography*—Van Dyke having to insert it in a footnote.

V *Final Bequests*

Upon Carnegie's death, when the will was opened, there remained $30 million to be dispersed—two-thirds of which went to the Carnegie Corporation of New York. The remaining $10 million went for yearly pensions to Dunfermline relatives, old friends and associates, one of whom was ex-President Taft. And attempting to shame the government into action, Carnegie had included Mrs. Theodore Roosevelt and Grover Cleveland's widow. The final million dollars went to Hampton Institute, the University of Pittsburgh, Stevens Institute, Cooper Union, the Relief Fund of the Authors Club of New York, and the St. Andrew's Society.[39]

There was no other monetary bequest—nothing more except for Carnegie's real estate. He wrote, "Having years ago made provision for my wife beyond her desires and ample enough to enable her to provide for our beloved daughter, Margaret, and being unable to judge at present what provision for our daughter will best promote her happiness, I leave to her mother the duty of providing for her as her mother deems best. A mother's love will be the best guide." At the time of his death, Louise Carnegie was sixty-two. She had known, approvingly, from the beginning that her husband planned to distribute the greatest part of his fortune to mankind. The entire Carnegie benefactions amounted to over $350 million—an overwhelming sum donated by one individual. Carnegie had given away 90 percent of his fortune within his lifetime. Believing to the end it was more blessed to give than to receive, the great benefactor had not died in disgrace.

VI *Significance*

The typical industrialist of a century ago was far from being the knowledgeable, suave, college-trained man of today's world—a public figure equally at home at an interview or on the speaker's platform, ready to give voice or pen to causes which may affect his business. Ordinarily he was a man of not more than average education; he had gone to work—often in his father's business or mill—in his teens and learned from older men or by experience. Very few, even up to the end of the nine-teenth century, could be accurately described as truly literate, much less learned men. If such a man used the pen it was likely to be in brief, brusque business letters, or as an accountant.

Andrew Carnegie quickly realized that writing was easily the most effective manner of getting his ideas and opinions before others, and that education was the key to influence, except for the bald, venal purchase of politicians and office holders, to which he would not stoop.

Many of his early business superiors gave him preferment and increased opportunity because they were impressed by what he wrote. But there is no reason to believe that it ever occurred to any of them to use his abilities in this respect for the benefit of their organizations. They looked on him as bright, ambitious, and capable, but as a little zany.

If not absolutely the first genuine writing industrialist, Car-negie was the first to use the full power of an interesting ap-proach, trenchant style, and broad knowledge and vocabulary in pushing his causes and making himself a public figure.

Newspaper editors—always likely to welcome "good copy" —were the first to recognize the value of what he had to say. His first two books, like the "story of my life" type of thing sometimes done by other successful men of his day, were writ-ten with the expectation of a very limited audience. But their greater interest and better style and content caught the eye of a publisher. And with the opportunity to get them before the public, Carnegie realized that his best way to success was by rewriting them. Other travel writers had used the pen to express their opinions and preferences; but few, if any, had deliberately used their works as a means to get their ideas and convictions a hearing, and to increase their influence in the world beyond their own circle. From the ashes of a defeat in his attempt to change the British opinion through organizing a newspaper chain, Carnegie set up a great publicity caper—his coaching trip throughout the length of England and Scotland. And when a chance opportunity came as a result, to get his name into the greatest of the English reviews, the article he wrote was eye-catching and controversial enough to attract international attention. From this time forward his pen was seldom idle, despite his busy life of making a vast fortune. Where another man's words might be listened to because he was a business leader, Carnegie was widely known as a writer before it was generally recognized that he was an industrial lion.

He was the first to set the precedent of furthering industry by influencing a wide segment of the public. The vocal and literary business leader or other public figure has appeared to a large degree because of the pattern that Carnegie set. And the ghost writer, a device which many later students have supposed him to have employed, has largely come into existence because of the challenging model he so successfully set.

One other extremely significant effect of Carnegie's writing was its strong contribution (illustrated by his career) to the public belief in the so-called "American dream"—that in a democratic, capitalist society any young man who was willing to work could achieve fame and fortune.

Notes and References

Chapter One

1. Andrew Carnegie to President Woodrow Wilson, January 23, 1915, in J. F. Wall, *Andrew Carnegie* (New York, 1970), p. 971.

2. *Autobiography of Andrew Carnegie*, ed. John C. Van Dyke (Boston, 1920), p. 13.

3. Wall, p. 83.

4. Letter to George Lauder, Sr., May 30, 1852; quoted in Burton J. Hendrick, *The Life of Andrew Carnegie* (New York, 1932), I, 45–49.

5. *Autobiography*, pp. 35–37.

6. Frank C. Harper, *Pittsburgh of Today* (New York, 1931), I, 330, 333.

7. *Autobiography*, p. 43; Hendrick, I, 58–59, gives the number as 1,800 and quotes the librarian as saying 2,000.

8. Quotations are taken from the text as given by Hendrick, I, 68–70, although even casual inspection shows that it is incomplete and probably corrupt as well. Unfortunately, no file of the *Dispatch* for this period appears to have been preserved.

9. [Margaret Barclay Wilson], "Carnegie Bibliography: List of Letters by Mr. [Andrew] Carnegie, Printed in Newspapers from March 18, 1895, to February 5, 1915, n.p. [Pittsburgh], n.d. [1930]; TS in Carnegie Library of Pittsburgh.

10. Pet name for Lauder.

11. Quoted, Hendrick, I, pp. 66, 72–77.

12. *Autobiography*, pp. 68–69.

13. *Rules for the Government of the Pennsylvania Railroad Company's Telegraph* (Harrisburg, Pa., 1863). Its location since the Penn-Central Railroad bankruptcy and auction of assets is unknown.

14. A native son would have written "supper."

15. William B. Wilson, *History of the Pennsylvania Railroad Company, and Historical Sketches, etc.* (Philadelphia, 1899), p. 117; but concerning this period Wilson was writing from hearsay, and differs widely from other biographical accounts.

16. Witness the selections in William B. Wilson, *Robert Pitcairn,*

1836–1909, in Memoriam (n.p., n.d. [1913]), 8–12, 19–22, in which Pitcairn's sentence length averages nearly fifty words.

17. *Autobiography*, p. 66.

18. The others include *Problems of Today* (New York, 1908), *The Empire of Business* (London and New York, 1903), and *James Watt* (Edinburgh and London, n.d. [1905]).

Chapter Two

1. Wall, pp. 203–204.

2. Ibid. p. 227.

3. Ibid. pp. 250–51.

4. Ibid. p. 152.

5. *Autobiography*, p. 93.

6. For example, he remarked in passing up the excursion to Switzerland: "I have seen enough mountain scenery in Scotland to satisfy me for a time." Letter to Margaret Morrison Carnegie, September 2, 1865; cited in Wall, pp. 231–32.

7. Hendrick, I, 137.

8. Bayard Taylor, *Views A-Foot*, second ed. (Philadelphia, n.d. [1848]), Preface by N. P. Willis, pp. 9–12.

9. *Autobiography*, p. 137.

10. For example, "If I had time, I would write frequently for the *Commercial* but there is none"; Paris, September 29, 1865. "I have an abundance for many letters to the *Commercial* and would like to write them, but where's the time?"; Verona, December 10, 1865. Travel letters in the possession of Margaret Carnegie Miller; TS, lent by J. F. Wall, as were the further Miller letters cited below.

11. Letter of September 25, 1865; in the possession of Margaret Carnegie Miller.

12. It is uncertain whether Carnegie drew this reference from Voltaire or Swift (by 1865 he was probably familiar with both writers) or from some intermediate source.

13. Andrew Carnegie to Margaret Morrison Carnegie and Thomas Carnegie, November 5 and 12, 1865; in the possession of Margaret Carnegie Miller.

14. Andrew Carnegie to Margaret Morrison Carnegie and Thomas Carnegie, May 25, 1865; in the possession of Margaret Carnegie Miller.

15. J. K. Winkler, *Incredible Carnegie* (New York, 1931), p. 103.

16. Winkler, p. 105, referring to these sales, says, "Some of these turned out to be worthless as autumn leaves." Unless the pronoun

refers to American bonds in general, there appears to be no truth in the statement. The principal reason Carnegie found selling easy was the confidence of bankers that his offerings were always sound.

17. Wall, p. 400.

18. Hendrick, I, illustration between pp. 146 and 147.

19. Wall, p. 364.

20. Andrew Carnegie, *Before the Nineteenth Century Club upon The Aristocracy of the Dollar* (n.p., n.d.); pamphlet in Carnegie Library of Pittsburgh.

21. Wall, p. 362. Carnegie's statement in the *Autobiography*, p. 145, that the meeting came through Anne C. L. Botta is evidently a slip in an aging man's memory. He had written in 1893 in "Characteristics," *Memoirs of Anne C. L. Botta*, p. 166, that Palmer had introduced him to her.

22. *Autobiography*, pp. 144–45.

23. Van Wyck Brooks, *The Confident Years* (New York, 1952), p. 6.

24. Despite references to the contrary in *Autobiography*, p. 327 (followed by Hendrick, I, 238), Wall, p. 362, is almost certainly correct in his conclusion that these men had little if any impact on Carnegie until after he moved to New York.

25. Andrew Carnegie, "Characteristics," in *Memoirs of Anne C. L. Botta, Written by her Friends, etc.,* ed. Vincenzo Botta (New York, 1894), p. 165.

26. Ibid.

27. Ibid., p. 166.

28. Ibid., p. 165.

29. Hendrick, I, 221–22.

30. Ibid., I, 239–40.

31. *Autobiography*, p. 322.

Chapter Three

1. Hendrick, I, 137.

2. Andrew Carnegie, *Round the World* (n.p., 1879), dedication.

3. Andrew Carnegie, *Our Coaching Trip* (New York, 1882), dedication.

4. *Autobiography*, pp. 203–204.

5. The similarity in type, makeup, and binding makes it appear that *Round the World*, like *Our Coaching Trip*, was printed as a favor by Charles Scribner's Sons.

6. Wall, p. 362.

7. *Round the World*, pp. 228–29.

8. Although he had evidently planned to be away a year, Carnegie returned to New York exactly eight months from the time he had sailed from San Francisco.

9. "Vandy" was John Vandevort, a boyhood friend and associate; "Harry" was Henry Phipps, Jr., another of the Homestead and European tour group.

10. *Autobiography*, pp. 200–201.

11. *Round the World*, p. 187.

12. Ibid., p. 22.

13. Ibid., p. 24.

14. *Round the World*, second ed. (New York, 1884), p. 4. Further references to this work will be found in the text in parentheses.

15. Winkler, p. 151.

16. *Autobiography*, p. 199.

17. *Our Coaching Trip*, title page.

18. Ibid., table following p. 275.

19. Ibid., p. 9.

20. Wall, pp. 401–403.

21. *Our Coaching Trip*, pp. 186–239. Further citations of this work are provided in parentheses in the text.

22. See above, p. 42.

23. *Autobiography*, pp. 203–204.

24. Ibid., p. 204.

25. Ibid.

26. Andrew Carnegie, *An American Four-in-Hand in Britain* (New York, 1883), pp. vii–viii.

27. Hendrick, I, 237.

28. See above, p. 45.

29. Compare *Round the World*, p. 2, and *Round the World*, second edition, p. 2.

30. Compare *Round the World*, p. 37, and *Round the World*, second edition, p. 44.

31. Carnegie's implication (*Autobiography*, p. 198) that this book was published prior to *An American Four-in-Hand in Britain* is apparently the result of a faulty memory.

32. Hendrick, I, 237.

Chapter Four

1. Quoted by Hendrick, I, 264–65.

2. Ibid., I, 147.

3. Ibid., I, 261–73; Wall, pp. 429–41.

4. Andrew Carnegie, "As Others See Us," *Fortnightly Review* NS 31 (February 1, 1882), p. 156. Carnegie here appears to be trying to leave the impression that the suggestion came from William E. Gladstone, at that time Britain's prime minister. If such were the case it is doubtful if he would have avoided using the name, even if—as is quite likely—he had himself engineered the request, as he was later to do with a compliment from King Edward VII (Hendrick, II, 174). Hendrick, in a prefatory note to this article in *Miscellaneous Writings of Andrew Carnegie*, ed. Burton J. Hendrick (New York, 1933), suggests that the person was Lord Roseberry.

5. Ibid., p. 156. Further citations from this article are added in parentheses in the text.

6. Andrew Carnegie to Samuel Storey, January 3, 1883 (quoted by Hendrick, I, 267): "I've sent an article to Escott, of the Fortnightly."

7. Hendrick, II, 389, mistakenly states that the speech was before "the legislature of Pennsylvania." A recast version was given before that body in April of the same year.

8. See below, p. 94.

9. Hendrick, I, 351.

10. *Autobiography*, p. 204.

11. Quoted in Hendrick, II, 268.

12. The first two were in British reviews, and until 1890 the numbers were equal, four each in Britain and America. From this time the number originally appearing overseas declined (although all in prestigious publications) in relation to the total. In the final decade of the century sixteen appeared in this country, and ten in England, while after 1899 there were twenty-six in American magazines, eight in British journals.

13. The other participants were Thomas Wentworth Higginson, Murat Halstead, Horace Porter, Robert Collyer, James H. Eilson, and M. W. Hazeltine.

14. See below, p. 122.

15. Single quotation marks were perhaps connected with Carnegie's effort to promote simplified spelling. See below, p. 152.

16. Andrew Carnegie, "The Next Step—A League of Nations," *Outlook* 86 (May 25, 1907), 151–52, part of a symposium including President Theodore Roosevelt, Edward Everett Hale, Baron Estournelles de Constant, and Lyman Abbott.

17. October 17, 1905. Printed in pamphlet form by the Student Representative Council, St. Andrews (n.p., n.d. [1905]), for the

International Union (Boston, 1906), and reprinted by the New York Peace Society (1911).

18. *Nineteenth Century and After* 60 (August 1906), 224–33.

19. *Century* 80 (June 1910), 307–10.

20. *Cosmopolitan Student* 5 (June 1915), 333–34.

21. Hendrick, II, 171–72.

22. Ibid., pp. 170–71.

23. *Nineteenth Century and After* 55 (April 1904), 538–42.

24. Ibid., p. 538.

25. Ibid., pp. 541–42.

26. *Independent* 70 (June 1, 1911), 1183–92.

27. *Woman's Home Companion* 43 (March 1916), 19.

Chapter Five

1. See above, p. 54.

2. Wall, pp. 389–97.

3. Andrew Carnegie, *Triumphant Democracy, or Fifty Years March of the Republic* (New York and London, 1886). John C. Van Dyke, in a footnote, *Autobiography*, p. 318, erroneously gives the dates as "London, 1886; New York, 1888."

4. Andrew Carnegie, "Wealth," *North American Review* 148 (June 1889), 653–64, reprinted in the *Pall Mall Gazette* as "The Gospel of Wealth." Under this title it was widely printed in pamphlet form and with minor changes in a book of the same name. It created a tremendous impression, and has been repeatedly reissued, as recently as 1962.

5. M. G. Mulhall, *Balance Sheet of the World for Ten Years, 1870–1880,* (London, 1881).

6. *Autobiography,* pp. 318–19.

7. With Carnegie, the term "race" had nothing to do with the races of mankind, but referred to nationality and language, or loosely as a combination of heredity and culture. Specifically, he used it constantly for English-speaking peoples, and sometimes for those of Anglo-Saxon heritage.

8. *Triumphant Democracy,* pp. 18–19. Further citations of this work are provided in parentheses in the text.

9. Carnegie, although not a believer in revealed religion, was thoroughly familiar with the King James Version of the Bible, frequently using unstated references and unidentified phrases and quotations from it in his writing and speech: e.g., "unstable as water, thou shalt not excel," *Triumphant Democracy,* p. 27, quoting Genesis 49:4.

10. Matthew 7:20.

11. James 2:18.

12. The incorrect addition of "free" is derived from the Constitution of Massachusetts; the other misquotations are merely examples of Carnegie's loose method of quotation from memory.

13. John Bartlett, *Familiar Quotations*, Centennial edition (Boston, 1955), p. 891, lists the "shirtsleeves" maxim merely as "attributed to Andrew Carnegie," although it occurs three times in his published works; the other instances are in his *Memorial Address on William Chambers*, October 19, 1909, issued in pamphlet form and reprinted in *Miscellaneous Writings*, I, 209, and in the pamphlet of his address *The Aristocracy of the Dollar*.

14. Hendrick, I, 274.

15. Wall, p. 444.

16. *American Historical Review* 57 (April 1952) 707–709.

17. I have been unable to find that Bridge ever held such a post or title, or did such work except as mentioned below, p. 79. He made no such claim.

18. *Our Coaching Trip*, p. 22; *Four-in-Hand*, p. 28.

19. Joseph F. Wall, Carnegie's definitive biographer, agrees with this statement (conversation with the author, 1970), as does Robert L. Beisner, *Twelve Against Empire* (New York, 1968), p. 281.

20. "Triumphant Democracy," rev. of Andrew Carnegie, *Triumphant Democracy, Saturday Review* 62 (September 18, 1886), 394.

21. Information taken from two unidentified clippings pasted in a copy of the first British edition in the present author's collection, one dated in pen, "Nov. 1887."

22. Andrew Carnegie, *Triumphant Democracy Ten Years Afterward, or Sixty Years March of the Republic* (New York, 1893).

23. See above, pp. 77–78.

24. Andrew Carnegie, *The Gospel of Wealth and Other Timely Essays* (New York, 1900); see below, Chapter Six, passim.

25. Ibid., pp. 159–60.

Chapter Six

1. See above, p. 33.

2. William E. Gladstone, *Diary*, July 13, 1887; cited by Hendrick, I, p. 318.

3. "Adam Smith, who did for the science of economics what Watt did for steam"; Andrew Carnegie, *James Watt* (Edinburgh and London, 1905) p. 29.

4. Andrew Carnegie, "My Experience with and Views upon the Tariff," *Century* 77 (December 1908), 196–205.

5. Andrew Carnegie, "The Worst Banking System in the World," *Outlook* 88 (February 29, 1908), 487–89.

6. Wall, p. 960.

7. Andrew Carnegie, "The Manchester School and Today." *Nineteenth Century*, February 1898.

8. Andrew Carnegie, "The Best Fields for Philanthropy," *North American Review* 149 (December 1889), 682.

9. Andrew Carnegie, *The Gospel of Wealth and Other Timely Essays* (New York, 1900), pp. 1–2. Further citations of this work are provided in parentheses in the text.

10. "The Gospel of Wealth," rev. of Andrew Carnegie, *The Gospel of Wealth and Other Timely Essays, Outlook* 67 (March 9, 1901), 572.

11. "The Best Fields for Philanthropy," p. 682.

12. Quoted, *Gospel of Wealth*, p. 20.

13. Counting both "Wealth" and "The Best Fields for Philanthropy," which were merged in the book to form "The Gospel of Wealth."

14. See below, pp. 121–22.

15. William E. Gladstone, "Mr. Carnegie's 'Gospel of Wealth,' a Review and a Recommendation," *Nineteenth Century* 28 (November 1890), 677–93.

16. Hugh Price Hughes, Henry L. Manning, and Hermann Adler, "Irresponsible Wealth," *Nineteenth Century* 28 (December 1890), 876–900.

17. Originally printed in the *Century* 60 (May 1900), 143–49.

18. "The Gospel of Wealth," review; see above, p. 166 n. 10.

19. Andrew Carnegie, "British Pessimism," *Nineteenth Century and After* 49 (June 1901), 901–12.

20. *Autobiography*, p. 248; Wall, p. 797.

21. Andrew Carnegie, "The Gospel of Wealth—II," *North American Review* 183 (December 7, 1906), 1096–1106.

22. Andrew Carnegie, *The Empire of Business* (New York, 1902), p. 84.

23. Ibid., p. 117.

24. Hendrick, II, 268.

25. Andrew Carnegie, *Problems of Today, Wealth—Labor—Socialism* (New York, 1908), p. 165—quoting Karl Pearson, *The Ethic of Free Thought* (London, 1888), p. 445.

26. Ibid., p. 169.

27. Ibid., pp. 176–77.

Chapter Seven

1. *Our Coaching Trip*, pp. 28–29.

2. Wall, p. 448.

3. *Autobiography*, pp. 58–59.

4. Hendrick, I, 147.

5. Ibid., I, 247.

6. *Autobiography*, pp. 202–203.

7. *Our Coaching Trip*, p. 19. In repeating the story in *Four-in-Hand*, p. 25, Carnegie substituted "enunciation" for "pronunciation."

8. Hendrick, I, 246–47.

9. Burton J. Hendrick, ed., *Miscellaneous Writings of Andrew Carnegie* (New York, 1933), I, 78–125, 126–35, 176–85, 185–99, 200–13, 214–39, 240–62, 265–305; II, 1–17, 61–78, 81–87, 88–122, 203–18, 221–71, 272–88, 291–309. (This work, published as the ninth and tenth volumes of Burton J. Hendrick, ed., *Writings of Andrew Carnegie* [New York, 1933], is separately titled, and the volumes separately numbered, both on spine and title page.) Henceforth cited as *Writings*.

10. *Gospel of Wealth*, pp. 219–48; *Empire of Business*, pp. 3–18, 71–91, 125–50, 173–86, 189–225, 285–287, 291–300.

11. Andrew Carnegie, "Industrial Pennsylvania," December 18, 1900, *New York-Pennsylvania Society Year Book*, I, 33–36.

12. "Andrew Carnegie, "The Scotch-American," November 30, 1891, *St Andrew's Society Yearbook for 1892*, pp. 119–26.

13. Quoted in "Industrial Pennsylvania," p. 18.

14. "A League of Peace," October 17, 1905, *Writings*, II, 221–71.

15. " 'Honor' and International Arbitration," March 10, 1910, *Writings*, II, 272–88.

16. Ibid., introductory note, p. 272.

17. *Our Coaching Trip*, pp. 199–201.

18. Ibid., p. 236.

19. *Peterhead Free Library Speech*, August 8, 1891 (n.p., n.d.); pamphlet in Carnegie Library of Pittsburgh.

20. *Autobiography*, pp. 17–18.

21. Speech at Dingwall, Scotland, July 16, 1903, pp. 4–5. Quoted in James M. Swank, ed., *More Busy Days* (Philadelphia, 1903), pamphlet collection of Carnegie speeches, in author's collection.

22. Tain, Scotland, August 27, 1903, *More Busy Days*, pp. 30–32.

23. Kilmarnock, Scotland, September 5, 1903, *More Busy Days*, pp. 42, 44, 47.

24. Govan, Scotland, September 11, 1903, *More Busy Days*, pp. 65–66, 69, 71.

25. Waterford, Ireland, October 21, 1903, *More Busy Days*, pp. 83–85.

26. Limerick, Ireland, October 20, 1903, *More Busy Days*, pp. 96–99.

27. Cork, Ireland, October 22, 1903, *More Busy Days*, p. 113.

28. Barrow, England, September 1, 1903, *More Busy Days*, p. 132.

29. Cornerstone at Ayr speech, October 5, 1892; pamphlet in Carnegie Library of Pittsburgh.

30. *Gospel of Wealth*, p. 248. Address at Glasgow, September 13, 1887. The quotation is from Tennyson's "Locksley Hall," and as usual is inexact.

31. Speech to graduating class, Bellevue Hospital, New York, March 9, 1885; pamphlet in author's collection.

32. "The Road to Business Success," Curry Commercial College, June 23, 1885. *Empire of Business*, pp. 3–18.

33. *Empire of Business*, p. 4; *Writings*, I, 261.

34. *Empire of Business*, p. 17.

35. "Wealth and Its Uses," *Empire of Business*, p. 125.

36. "Business," *Empire of Business*, p. 193.

37. "The Industrial Ascendancy of the World," *Writings*, I, 78–125.

38. Ibid., p. 79.

39. Ibid., pp. 120–22.

40. "A Confession of Religious Faith," *Writings*, II, 291–319. Further references to this speech are inserted in parentheses in the text.

41. "White and Black in the South," *Writings*, II, 81–87.

42. "The Negro in America," *Writings*, II, 88–122.

43. Wall, pp. 973–76. Wall erroneously states (p. 976) that Hendrick omitted this speech from his edition of Carnegie's works.

44. *Writings*, II, 120–22.

45. "Old Scotland and New England," *Writings*, I, 126–35.

46. *The Aristocracy of the Dollar*, c. 1883, Nineteenth Century Club; pamphlet in Carnegie Library of Pittsburgh.

47. "Pittsburgh and Its Future," address before the Pittsburgh Chamber of Commerce, November 10, 1898; *Chamber 1899 Yearbook*, Carnegie Library of Pittsburgh.

Chapter Eight

1. For example, in regard to the nonexistent cable from the union at Homestead, *Autobiography*, p. 223; Wall, pp. 575–76.

2. *Letters of Richard Watson Gilder* (New York, 1916), p. 374; cited in *Autobiography*, p. 280.

3. Ibid., p. 375; cited in *Autobiography*, p. 328.

4. *Autobiography*, Editor's Note, p. ix.

5. Ibid., preface, p. v.

6. Hendrick, I, 415–16. This first section appears to have ended with p. 209, line 5, of the Riverside Press edition. The next paragraph begins a section apparently written in 1907, but the subsequent text gives evidence of numerous revisions.

7. Wall, pp. 139–40.

8. *Triumphant Democracy*, p. 297.

9. *Autobiography*, p. 297. Further citations of the *Autobiography* are provided in parentheses in the text.

10. *James Watt*, p. 5.

11. Ibid., p. 12. Further citations of *James Watt* in this chapter are provided in parentheses in the text.

12. *Autobiography*, 12, 37.

13. The quotation is a paraphrase from Scott's *Lady of the Lake.*

14. James Patrick Muirhead, *Life of James Watt* (London, 1858), p. 18.

15. *Autobiography*, p. 33.

16. Muirhead, pp. 25–26.

17. "William Chambers," *Writings*, I, 200–13; "Stanton the Patriot," ibid., I, 215–39; "Ezra Cornell," ibid., I, 240–62.

18. Delivered at Kenyon College on Memorial Day 1906. Following the *Ohio Archaeological and Historical Quarterly*, in which the speech was printed (15, pp. 291–311), Hendrick titles it "Stanton the Patriot." Originally (pamphlet, Kenyon College, 1906, in Carnegie Library of Pittsburgh) it simply bore the subject's name.

19. *Autobiography*, p. 66.

20. *Writings*, I, 256–57.

21. The speech was delivered October 19, 1909, at Peebles, Scotland, at the jubilee of the Chambers Institution.

22. *Memoirs*, p. 165.

23. Elizabeth Nitchie, *The Criticism of Literature* (New York, 1928), p. 259.

24. Really nineteenth. Carnegie fails to realize that Old Style (Julian calendar) dating, by which the new year began with March,

was used in Britain until 1750. Virtually all writers on Watt have fallen into the same error, especially in regard to his age at death. Ivor B. Hart, *James Watt and the History of Steam Power* (New York, 1949), says (p. 231) that Watt died "in his eighty-fourth year," instead of eighty-third. Carnegie (*James Watt*, p. 146) speaks of him at death as "aged eighty-three." Even Muirhead (p. 511), who should have known better, in contradicting Walter Scott's statement that Watt was "in his eighty-fifth year" at the time of a visit to Scotland in 1817, makes it read "eighty-second." At his death, August 19, 1819, Watt was exactly eighty-two years, seven months of age. If there were any doubt that his birth was in January 1736 Old Style—1737 New Style—it is dispelled by the notes he sent to friends early in 1819 with busts he had made after perfecting a mechanism for copying, in which he describes them as "the work of a young artist just entering his eighty-third year" (*Encyclopaedia Britannica* [1954] 23, p. 437). Watt would not have forgotten the difference between the Gregorian and Julian dating.

25. *James Watt*, p. 27.

26. *Autobiography*, p. 105.

27. *James Watt*, p. 94.

28. Ibid., p. 137; *Writings*, I, 254; *Autobiography*, p. 51.

29. *James Watt*, p. 142. (Carnegie was almost seventy when he wrote this.)

30. The notable and praiseworthy exception is Wall.

31. Nitchie, p. 256.

32. Ibid., p. 250.

33. Ibid., p. 260.

34. Ibid., p. 264.

Chapter Nine

1. Andrew Carnegie to Henry Holt, February 25, 1915; quoted by Wall, p. 893.

2. Andrew Carnegie to Margaret Morrison and Thomas Carnegie, 1865–1866; Margaret Carnegie Miller collection.

3. Quoted in Hendrick, II, 287–88.

4. Quoted, ibid., pp. 285–87.

5. See above, p. 37.

6. Letter to Trustees, Carnegie Peace Fund, December 14, 1910. Pamphlet (n.p., n.d.), Carnegie Library of Pittsburgh.

7. Quoted in Hendrick, II, 68.

8. Wall, p. 664.

9. Hendrick, II, 69.

10. Quoted in Hendrick, II, 311–13.

11. See above, pp. 63–64.

12. Quoted in Hendrick, II, 310–11.

13. *Autobiography*, p. 357. I am totally at a loss to explain Hendrick's changes from the original in quoting the passage; Hendrick, II, 314.

14. See above, pp. 19–20.

15. Adapting Milton's "To the Lord General Cromwell."

16. Wall, p. 1024.

Chapter Ten

1. Evidently the end of 1870. See above, p. 33.

2. Hendrick, I, 268.

3. Wall, pp. 720–33.

4. Ibid., pp. 792, 789.

5. "Steel Manufacturing in the United States in the Nineteenth Century," Review of the Century number, *New York Post*, January 12, 1901, and "The Woman as Queen." Hendrick, II, 391, lists this as " 'The Woman in the Queen,' *Review of Reviews*, February, 1901," and in *Writings* (I, 186) as " 'Queen Victoria,' *Review of the Republic*, February, 1901." It is not to be found in either the British or American *Review of Reviews*, and the *Union List of Periodicals* does not include any *Review of the Republic*.

6. To Hayne Davis, *Among the World's Peacemakers* (New York, 1907).

7. Theodore Roosevelt, *The Roosevelt Policy, Speeches, Letters and State Papers, Relating to Corporate Wealth etc.* (New York, 1908).

8. Ibid., pp. ix–xxi, signature at end. Further citations from this introduction are inserted in parentheses in the text.

9. "Review of *The Roosevelt Policy*," (London) *Times Literary Supplement*, July 16, 1908, p. 228; quoted by Wall, p. 970.

10. See above, p. 98.

11. See above, p. 84.

12. Wall, p. 880.

13. *Autobiography*, p. 245.

14. Wall, pp. 830, 815.

15. Hendrick, II, 277.

16. Ibid., I, 352–64.

17. Wall, p. 828.

18. Hendrick, II, 203.

19. Wall, p. 819.

20. Ibid., p. 832; Hendrick, II, 229.

21. Hendrick, II, 260.

22. *Autobiography*, p. 247.

23. Hendrick, II, 253–54; Wall, p. 864.

24. Wall, pp. 859–63.

25. Hendrick, II. 332–34.

26. Wall, pp. 871–80.

27. Ibid., 836–37.

28. *Autobiography*, p. 266.

29. Wall, pp. 891–93.

30. Ibid., pp. 904–11.

31. Hendrick, II, 353.

32. *Autobiography*, p. 278; Hendrick, II, 353.

33. Hendrick, II, 359.

34. Wall, pp. 409, 805, 854.

35. *Autobiography*, p. 278.

36. Wall, p. 847.

37. Hendrick, II, 162–63.

38. Wall, pp. 882–83.

39. Ibid., pp. 1042–43. For a further account of the will, see the *New York Times*, August 29, 1919, p. 1.

Selected Bibliography

PRIMARY SOURCES

1. Collected Works

Andrew Carnegie's College Lectures etc. Ed. Daniel Butterfield. New York: F. T. Neely, 1896.
Three Busy Weeks etc. Comp. A. S. Cunningham. Dunfermline: W. Clark and Son, 1902. Nine Carnegie speeches.
More Busy Days etc. Ed. James M. Swank. Philadelphia: Allen, Lane and Scott, 1903. Eight Carnegie Speeches.
A Carnegie Anthology. Comp. Margaret B. Wilson. New York: privately printed, 1915.
Writings of Andrew Carnegie, 10 vols. Ed. Burton J. Hendrick. New York: Doubleday, Page and Co., 1933.
Letters of Andrew Carnegie and Louise Whitfield. Ed. Helen H. Dow. New York: no publisher, 1956.

2. Books or Parts of Books

Rules for the Government of the Pennsylvania Railroad Company's Telegraph. Harrisburg, Pa.: no publisher, 1863.
Round the World. [New York]: [Charles Scribner's Sons?], 1879.
Our Coaching Trip. [New York]: [Charles Scribner's Sons], 1882.
An American Four-in-Hand in Britain. New York: Charles Scribner's Sons, 1883.
Round the World (revised and enlarged). New York: Charles Scribner's Sons, 1884.
Triumphant Democracy, or Fifty Years' March of the Republic. New York: Charles Scribner's Sons; London: Sampson Low, Marston, Searle and Rivington, 1886.
"From Andrew Carnegie," *Courtlandt Palmer*, ed. F. W. Christen. New York: Nineteenth Century Club, 1889.
Triumphant Democracy Ten Years Afterward, or Sixty Years' March of the Republic. New York: Charles Scribner's Sons, 1893.
"Characteristics," in *Memoirs of Anne C. L. Botta*, ed. Vincenzo Botta. [New York]: no publisher, 1893.

"Genius Illustrated from Burns," *Liber Scriptorum*. New York: The Authors' Club, 1893.

The Gospel of Wealth and Other Timely Essays. New York: Century, 1900.

"The South African Question," in James Bryce, et als. *Briton and Boer, Both Sides of the South African Question*. New York and London: Harper and Brothers, 1900.

The Empire of Business. New York and London: Harper and Brothers, 1903.

James Watt. Famous Scots Series No. 42. Edinburgh and London: Oliphant, Anderson and Ferrier, 1905.

Problems of Today, Wealth, Labor, Socialism. New York: Doubleday, Page and Co., 1908.

Autobiography of Andrew Carnegie. Ed. John C. Van Dyke. Boston: Houghton, Mifflin Co., 1920.

A. Introductions

CHITTENDEN, HIRAM M. *War or Peace*. Chicago: A. C. McClurg and Co.; London: Sampson and Low, 1911.

DAVIS, HAYNE. *Among the World's Peacemakers*. New York: Progressive Press, 1907.

ROOSEVELT, THEODORE. *The Roosevelt Policy*. New York: Current Literature, 1908.

B. Edited

CARNEGIE, ANDREW, ed. *Business*. Boston: Hall and Locke Co.

3. Magazine Articles

"As Others See Us," *Fortnightly Review*, NS 31, (February 1, 1882) 156–65.

"The McKinley Bill," *Nineteenth Century*, 29 (June 1891), 1027–36.

"Imperial Federation, An American View" *Nineteenth Century*, 30 (September 1891), 490–508.

"A Look Ahead," *North American Review*, 156 (June 1893) 685–710.

"The Silver Problem, A Word to Wage Earners," *North American Review*, 157 (September 1893) 354–70.

"The Value of the World's Fair to the American People," *Engineering Magazine*, 6 (January, 1894) 417–22.

"How I Became a Millionaire," *Cassell's Family Magazine*, Series 4, 19 (May 1896) 450–56.

"The Ship of State Adrift," *North American Review*, 162 and 163 (June and October 1896) 641–48, 496–503.

"Mr. Bryan as a Conjuror," *North American Review*, 164 (January 1897) 106–18.

"The Presidential Election—Our Duty, Bryan or McKinley?" *North American Review*, 171 (October 1900), 495–507.

"The Opportunity of the United States," *North American Review*, 174 (May 1902), 606–12.

"Britain's Appeal to the Gods," *Nineteenth Century and After*, 55 (April 1904), 538–42.

"The Anglo-French-American Understanding," *North American Review*, 181 (October 1905), 510–17.

"The Cry of 'Wolf,'" *Nineteenth Century and After*, 60 (August 1906), 224–33.

"The Gospel of Wealth—II," *North American Review*, 183 (December 1906), 1096–1106.

"The Next Step—A League of Nations," *Outlook*, 86 (May 25, 1907), 151–52.

"The Second Chamber," *Nineteenth Century and After*, 62 (November 1907), 689–98.

"The Laird of Briarcliff Manor," *Outlook*, 89 (May 16, 1908),107–11.

"Peace Versus War—The President's Solution," *Century*, 80 (June 1910), 307–16.

"Tribute to Mark Twain," *North American Review*, 191 (June 1910), 827–28.

"Dr. Golf," *Independent*, 70 (June 1, 1911), 1183–92.

"Arbitration," *Contemporary Review*, 100 (August 1911), 169–76.

"The Industrial Problem," *North American Review*, 194 (December 1911), 914–20.

"A Silver Lining to the War Cloud," *The World Today*, 21 (February 1912), 1792a.

"Hereditary Transmission of Property," *Century*, 87 (January 1914), 441–43.

"The Decadence of Militarism," *Contemporary Student*, 5 (June 1915), 333–34.

4. Published Addresses

The Aristocracy of the Dollar, Nineteenth Century Club, 1883(?). Pamphlet, n.p., n.d.

[Untitled] *to Medical Students, Bellevue Hospital*, March 9, 1885. Pamphlet, n.p., n.d.

Some Facts About the American Republic, Dundee, Scotland, March 18, 1889. Pamphlet, n.p., n. d.

The Future of Pittsburgh, Pittsburgh Chamber of Commerce, Nov. 19, 1898. Pittsburgh: Chamber of Commerce Yearbook, 1899.

The Future of Labor. American Academy of Political and Social Science, 1909. Pamphlet, n.p., n.d.

Aberdeen University Rectorial Address, June 6, 1912. Pamphlet, n.p., n.d.

SECONDARY SOURCES

ALDERSON, BERNARD. *Andrew Carnegie*. New York: Doubleday, Page and Co., 1902. Strictly sycophant work.

Andrew Carnegie Centenary. New York: Carnegie Corporation of New York, 1935. Tributes and recollections by prominent men who knew Carnegie.

ARBUTHNOT, THOMAS S. *Heroes of Peace*. [Pittsburgh]: n.p., 1935. A charming account of the origin and spirit of the Carnegie Hero Fund.

BEISNER, R. L. *Twelve Against Empire*. New York: McGraw-Hill, 1968. Good essay on Carnegie's fight against annexing the Philippines, and similar national actions.

BRIDGE, J. H. *Inside History of the Carnegie Steel Co*. New York: Aldine, 1903. Principally concerned with the Carnegie-Frick estrangement, with strong anti-Carnegie bias.

BROOKS, VAN WYCK. *The Confident Years*. New York: Dutton, 1952. Good background study of the era of Carnegie's principal activity.

BRUCE, ROBERT V. *1877—Year of Violence*. Indianapolis: Bobbs-Merrill, 1959. A good study of industry in Carnegie's early period of activity.

CHAMPLIN, JOHN D. *Chronicle of the Coach*. New York: Charles Scribner's Sons, 1886. Background history on Carnegie's first successful book.

HACKER, LOUIS M. *The World of Andrew Carnegie*. Philadelphia: Lippincott, 1968. Fine background material on Carnegie's business years.

HARPER, FRANK C. *Pittsburgh of Today, Its Resources and People*. New York: American Historical Society, 1931. City background.

HARVEY, GEORGE. *Henry Clay Frick, the Man*. New York: Charles Scribner's Sons, 1928. Sycophantic biography of Carnegie's principal later aide, and worst enemy. Strongly biased against Carnegie.

HENDRICK, BURTON J. *The Life of Andrew Carnegie*, two vols. Garden City, N.Y.: Doubleday, 1932. Done to please Carnegie's family.
————, and HENDERSON, DANIEL. *Louise Whitfield Carnegie*. New York: Hastings House, 1950. In praise of Carnegie's wife.
HILL, NAPOLEON. *Think and Grow Rich*. Cleveland: Ralston Co., 1937. Claims to be based on Carnegie's talks with writer.
HOLBROOK, STEWART. *Iron Brew*. New York: MacMillan, 1939. Material on steel industry strikes and labor problems.
HUGHES, JONATHAN. *The Vital Few*. New York: Houghton, Mifflin, 1965. Fifty good pages on Carnegie as one of the great forces in American industrial progress.
LESTER, R. M. *Forty Years of Carnegie Giving*. New York: Charles Scribner's Sons, 1941. A summary of benefactions.
LYNCH, FREDERICK. *Personal Recollections of Andrew Carnegie*. New York: Fleming H. Revell, 1920. Good material on Carnegie's cultural attitudes.
McCLOSKEY, R. G. *American Conservatism in the Age of Enterprise*. Cambridge, Mass.: Harvard University Press, 1951. Good presentation of Carnegie's place in America of his day.
MULHALL, M. G. *Balance Sheet of the World for Ten Years, 1870–1880*. London: Edward Stanford, 1881. Gazetteer of international statistics which gave Carnegie the idea and much material for *Triumphant Democracy*.
NEVIN, R. P. *Les Trois Rois*. Pittsburgh: Eichbaum, 1888. Earliest and most worshipful biographical notice of Carnegie, by a friend. Compares his career with those of two other Pittsburghers, William Thaw and George Westinghouse.
PELLING, HENRY. *America and the British Left, from Bright to Bevan*. London: A. and C. Black, 1956. Excellent brief coverage of Carnegie's moves in British politics.
Perspectives on Peace, 1910–1960. London: Carnegie Endowment for International Peace, 1960. Summary of Peace Fund work.
SPENCER, HERBERT. *Autobiography*. New York: D. Appleton, 1904. Material on friendship with Carnegie.
STEAD, W. T. "Mr. Carnegie's Conundrum," *Review of Reviews Annual*. London: Review of Reviews Corporation, 1900. In view of Carnegie's liquidation of his industrial holdings, a fellow liberal wonders if and how the millionaire will carry out his charitable plans.
WALL, JOSEPH F. *Andrew Carnegie*. New York: Oxford University Press, 1970. At long last an honest and definitive Carnegie biography.

WILLIAMS, HARLEY. *Men of Stress*. London: Jonathan Cape, 1948.
Study of the ambivalent personalities of Carnegie, Lord Lever-
hulme, and Woodrow Wilson.
WINKLER, J. K. *Incredible Carnegie*. Garden City, N.Y.: Garden City
Publishing Co., 1931. Charmingly written hatchet job.

Index